7385 7400

Dr. E's Super Stellar

SOLAR SYSTEM

Dr. E's Super Stellar

SOLAR SYSTEM

Massive Mountains! Supersize Storms! Alien Atmospheres!

Bethany Ehlmann
with **Jennifer Swanson**

CONTENTS

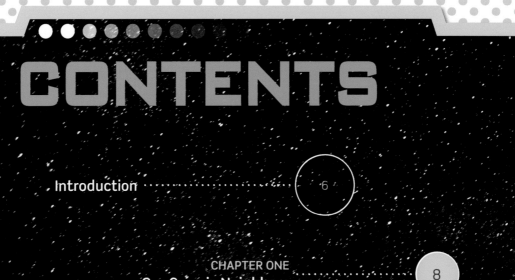

Introduction 6

CHAPTER ONE
Our Cosmic Neighbors 8

CHAPTER TWO
Dwarf Planets, Meteors, Asteroids, and Comets 20

CHAPTER THREE
Planets 32

CHAPTER FOUR
Frozen Worlds 42

CHAPTER FIVE
Erosion and Weathering 50

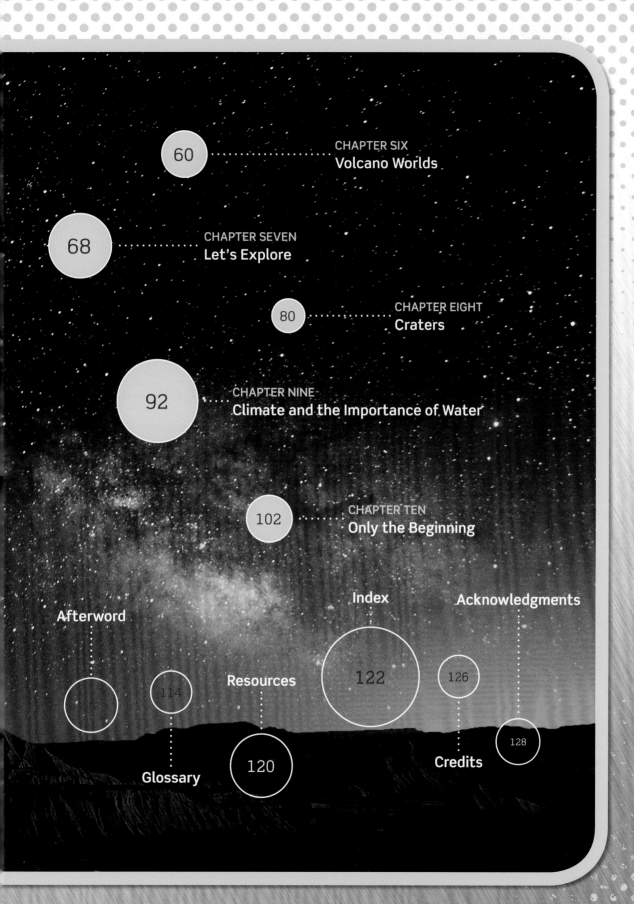

60 .... CHAPTER SIX
Volcano Worlds

68 .... CHAPTER SEVEN
Let's Explore

80 .... CHAPTER EIGHT
Craters

92 ...... CHAPTER NINE
Climate and the Importance of Water

102 ...... CHAPTER TEN
Only the Beginning

Afterword
112

Glossary
114

Resources
120

Index
122

Credits
126

Acknowledgments
128

INTRODUCTION

GREETINGS!

I'M DR. BETHANY EHLMANN. I'm a planetary geologist. I study rocks on Earth and on other planets in our solar system.

Here on Earth, I travel to some of the hottest, coldest, driest, and most acidic places on the globe. Exploring the geologic features and environmental conditions in these remote spots can help us figure out how to best tackle exploration elsewhere in our solar system, where conditions can be even more extreme.

Studying rocks on Earth also helps us learn about Mars. Mars and Earth are similar planets. Both have atmospheres of gases and a record of rocks stretching back to their beginning. We use these rocks to help us determine how both planets formed, and why Earth has life and Mars ... might!

Mars is my specialty. From right here on Earth, I help steer the NASA rover Curiosity across the surface of Mars to areas we might find interesting. I direct Curiosity to drive up to rocks and analyze the minerals within them. I am looking for clues about the planet's environment and how it has evolved over billions of years. The history of Mars is written in its rocks—particularly the history of its water.

This is exciting and fascinating work. But I've often wondered what it would be like if I could zoom around our solar system in person—like a superhero! And that's where the idea for the Dr. E comics came from.

In this book, you'll see me as Dr. E. My super sidekick, Rover, and I will be your tour guides as we explore our solar system and learn more about its planets, asteroids, moons, and stars. Along the way we will study how our solar system formed over billions of years and search for habitable environments. The comics in this book, like the superhero Dr. E, are fictional, of course. But the science is real. Get ready for takeoff!

DR. EHLMANN POSES WITH A NEAR
TWIN OF THE NASA ROVER CURIOSITY.
THIS TEST BED ROVER IS USED HERE
ON EARTH TO TRY OUT MANEUVERS
FOR THE REAL CURIOSITY ON MARS.

OUR COSMIC NEIGHBORS

OUR COSMIC NEIGHBORS

When you think of a solar system, what does it look like? Does it look like ours, with one sun, eight main planets, millions of asteroids, and five dwarf planets? Or does it look wildly different? Scientists have confirmed thousands of other planets around other stars. Hundreds of them may be Earthlike. If we could eventually study all the stars in our Milky Way galaxy alone, we might find billions of Earthlike exoplanets!

Take two systems within our own Milky Way galaxy, for example. Kepler-11 is a star like our sun with six planets orbiting it. All six planets are larger than Earth, and all of them orbit their star within a zone that is half the distance that Earth is from our sun. That's a lot of large planets in a relatively small zone! Or take the newly discovered TRAPPIST-1 system. It's far away from Earth—40 light-years (235 trillion miles; 378 trillion km) to be exact—but still within the Milky Way. The TRAPPIST-1 system has seven Earth-size rocky planets closely orbiting a dwarf star, which has a relatively cool temperature, in the constellation Aquarius. The TRAPPIST-1 system has so many rocky planets similar to ours that one might even host life, like our Earth. Scientists are especially excited about three of the planets. Like Earth, these three planets are not too close and not too far from their star. They orbit in what is called the "habitable zone."

In our own solar system, only Venus, Earth, and Mars occupy the habitable zone. It is sometimes nicknamed the "Goldilocks zone" after the fairy tale *Goldilocks and the Three Bears*. Temperatures in this zone are not too hot and not too cold. It's the perfect spot for liquid water to exist. Too close to the star, and the water would boil away. Too far from the

This system, Kepler-11, has a star like our sun and six planets. All six planets orbit within an area that is half the distance of Earth to our sun.

Our solar system has eight main planets.

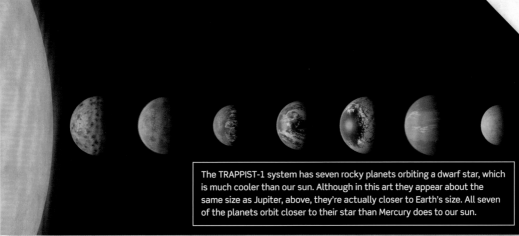

The TRAPPIST-1 system has seven rocky planets orbiting a dwarf star, which is much cooler than our sun. Although in this art they appear about the same size as Jupiter, above, they're actually closer to Earth's size. All seven of the planets orbit closer to their star than Mercury does to our sun.

star, and the water would freeze. The habitable zone allows water to remain a liquid, and that makes it just right for life as we know it. While Venus is too hot for liquid water and Mars is almost too cold for liquid water, on Earth, most of our water exists in liquid form. It's in our oceans and seas.

These conditions—the potential for liquid water; a rocky surface on which water could collect into lakes, oceans, and rivers; and comfortable temperatures—are all important ingredients for life as we know it to exist, grow, and thrive.

Exploring our cosmic neighborhood is exciting. We can search for the possibility that life could exist somewhere else in the universe. But that's not all. We can also consider questions about how our solar system formed, how planets work, and even the history of our home planet, Earth. Scientists are learning new things about our own solar system all the time. The more we study our home system, the more we learn about Earth, the universe, and our place in it.

FINDING PLANET NINE

We know that our solar system is home to eight planets, right? Well, two researchers from the California Institute of Technology (Caltech) beg to differ. They've found evidence that a giant ninth planet might be in the outer reaches of our solar system. Although no one has actually seen the planet yet, analyses of nearby objects' orbits and detailed computer modeling indicate there may be a large planet two times farther from the sun than Neptune. Who knows? We may be welcoming a new neighbor to the block pretty soon!

EXPLORING OUR NIGHT SKY

Humans have always explored the night sky. In the beginning, we just looked up at the twinkling lights in the dark sky. Then the invention of telescopes let us look closer to discover planets among the stars. Today, we've peered into the sky with high-tech telescopes and sent rovers and probes to planets, asteroids, and the outer edges of our home system. With each new advancement in exploration, we're learning new things and improving our understanding about how our solar system works.

Over the years, we've discovered new planets, we've classified and reclassified celestial bodies, and we've made predictions, which sometimes have turned out to be true and sometimes not true! Pluto was once considered a planet. Ceres was once considered an asteroid. Now both are called dwarf planets. There may be a ninth planet at the edge of our solar system. Yet there was a time when people did not even understand the most basic nature of our solar system.

IN THE DARK

Long ago, people didn't know that the sun was the center of our solar system. In the early second century, the Greek astronomer Ptolemy proposed that Earth was the center of the solar system. For more than 1,300 years, almost everyone accepted his theory. But in 1514, mathematician and astronomer Nicolaus Copernicus suggested that the solar system was centered on the sun. He theorized that the size of a planet's orbit, or path, depended upon its distance from the sun. Copernicus's idea was revolutionary and went against what people thought they knew. Many leaders rejected this theory because it was too different. There was no proof.

KONSTANTIN BATYGIN & MIKE BROWN

Dr. Konstantin Batygin, a professor at Caltech, was born in Russia and spent his elementary school years in Japan, where his father worked as a physicist at the RIKEN Institute. His graduate school work led him to the planetary science department at Caltech, where he met Mike Brown. Dr. Brown, a professor at Caltech, has been studying the edges of our solar system. After discovering Eris—which led to the debate about Pluto and finally the brand-new category of "dwarf planet"—Dr. Brown, together with Dr. Batygin, looked farther outward, finding perturbations in Kuiper belt object orbits. These two scientists are now leading the charge to locate the mysterious Planet Nine, which may be the cause of the perturbations.

Copernicus's model of the solar system put the sun in the center.

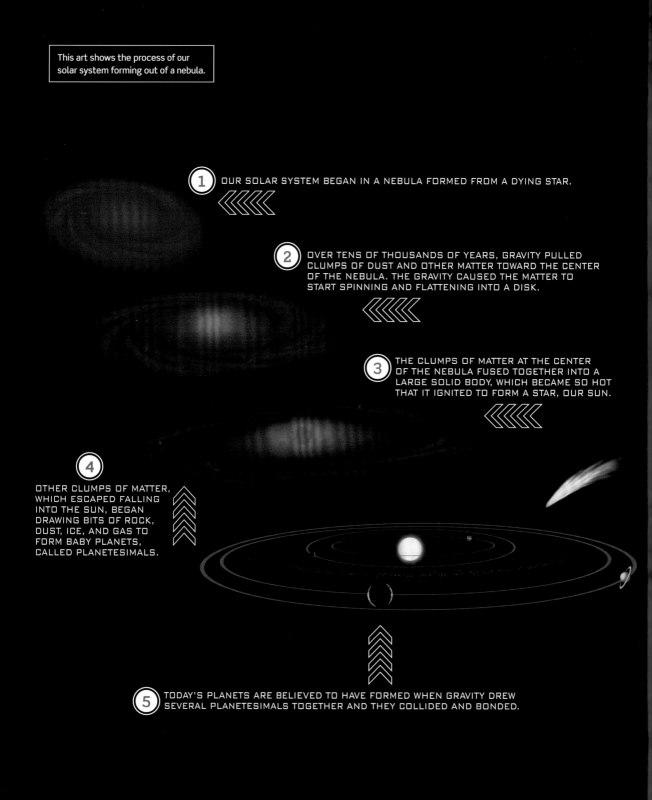

This art shows the process of our solar system forming out of a nebula.

① OUR SOLAR SYSTEM BEGAN IN A NEBULA FORMED FROM A DYING STAR.

② OVER TENS OF THOUSANDS OF YEARS, GRAVITY PULLED CLUMPS OF DUST AND OTHER MATTER TOWARD THE CENTER OF THE NEBULA. THE GRAVITY CAUSED THE MATTER TO START SPINNING AND FLATTENING INTO A DISK.

③ THE CLUMPS OF MATTER AT THE CENTER OF THE NEBULA FUSED TOGETHER INTO A LARGE SOLID BODY, WHICH BECAME SO HOT THAT IT IGNITED TO FORM A STAR, OUR SUN.

④ OTHER CLUMPS OF MATTER, WHICH ESCAPED FALLING INTO THE SUN, BEGAN DRAWING BITS OF ROCK, DUST, ICE, AND GAS TO FORM BABY PLANETS, CALLED PLANETESIMALS.

⑤ TODAY'S PLANETS ARE BELIEVED TO HAVE FORMED WHEN GRAVITY DREW SEVERAL PLANETESIMALS TOGETHER AND THEY COLLIDED AND BONDED.

Fortunately, the idea of a heliocentric, or sun-centered, solar system was not completely discarded. Italian astronomer Galileo Galilei and then Danish scientist Tycho Brahe set out to study the solar system with telescopes. Brahe mapped the movement of a comet and was the first to prove it was a faraway celestial body rather than something in our atmosphere. Over many decades, Brahe also kept careful record of the planets as they traveled across the sky. He also identified and observed a comet that he figured out was farther from the Earth than the moon.

Later, Johannes Kepler combined the data gathered by Brahe with his own data, and used mathematics to create the laws of planetary motion. These laws describe how items in the solar system move. They place the sun in the center of our solar system, explain why the planets move the way they do, and explain how their orbits are affected by their position from the sun.

THE FORMATION OF HOME

Today, we know that the solar system is heliocentric. We know the planets, their moons, and other objects. We even know how our solar system was created.

Imagine the universe in its youngest days. Stars are born, live, and die. One day, more than eight billion years after the universe began, *boom!* One or more stars in our home galaxy, the Milky Way, went supernova, breaking apart in explosions. Hot bits of dust and gas particles extended outward to space.

Gradually, the bits of matter cooled, and began to clump together within clouds called nebulae. These clouds were the beginnings of solar systems. About 4.6 billion years ago, our own solar system started to form from one of these nebulae.

THE TERM "HELIOCENTRIC" COMES FROM COMBINING THE ANCIENT GREEK WORD HELIOS, MEANING SUN, AND CENTRIC, WHICH IS FROM THE GREEK WORD KENTRIKOS, MEANING CENTER.

Over tens of thousands of years, gravity pulled the clumps of dust and matter toward the center of the nebula. As they compressed in the center, they heated up, forming into a more solid shape, our sun.

As the clumps of matter that were scattered throughout the nebula moved toward the center, toward our young sun, their movement created a churning effect. As the nebula churned, it began to rotate in one direction, much like a spinning top. The spinning continued, and the nebula flattened out into a flat plane, or disk, with our sun in the center.

Some of the matter escaped falling into the sun. It began to clump together, drawing bits of rock, dust, ice, and gas. These clumps became the beginnings of tiny new planets. These baby planets are called planetesimals.

Today's planets are believed to have formed when gravity drew several planetesimals together and they collided and bonded. After only a few million years, our amazing solar system had formed.

Our solar system contains eight planets,
five dwarf planets, and millions of asteroids all orbiting around our fiery sun.

KEY
BROWN ORBITS: **the rocky planets (Mercury, Venus, Earth, Mars)**   BLUE ORBIT: **the asteroid belt and dwarf planet Ceres**
GREEN ORBITS: **the gas giants (Jupiter, Saturn, Uranus, Neptune)**   PURPLE ORBITS: **the Kuiper belt dwarf planets (Pluto, Haumea, Makemake, Eris)**   *Planets and orbits not to scale

YOU LIGHT UP MY LIFE

So what does our solar system look like? We have the sun, of course, which is the biggest and most massive object in our solar system. But even though we think it's huge, our sun is actually only a medium-size star in the universe. Scientists classify our sun as a yellow dwarf star, which means it's smack-dab in the middle of the star size chart.

Like an orange, the sun is almost perfectly round, and is more than 864,938 miles (1.392 million km) across. That is the width of almost 109 Earths lined up right next to each other.

The sun is also hot. Really hot! At its core, it has temperatures of up to 27 million °F (15 million °C). These extremely high temperatures make possible the nuclear fusion reaction that gives the sun its energy. It is that intense heat that keeps our planet—and the rest of our solar system—warm. The sun has different layers, and as you go farther out from the core, the temperatures drop. The surface of the sun, called the photosphere, sends light our way. It is a relatively cool 10,000°F (5500°C), but still far too hot for any human to explore.

MEET THE NEIGHBORS

While it is certainly the most massive, the sun is not the only important object in our solar system. Millions of asteroids and comets—masses of dust and gas—and, oh yes, the eight planets can also be found there. Closest to the sun are four rocky planets: Mercury, Venus, Earth, and Mars. Mercury is the smallest planet and the one closest to the sun. Venus and Earth are similar in size, but Mars is about half the diameter of Earth.

The four outer planets are Jupiter, Saturn, Uranus, and Neptune. They are called gas giants and are mostly composed of hydrogen, helium, and other types of gases. Jupiter is the largest of all of the planets in our solar system, with Saturn being a close second in size. Uranus and Neptune are smaller, but still more than four times larger than Venus or Earth.

In between the planets is space, but it's not completely empty. Asteroids, comets, and gases fill up some of those areas. In fact, if you look between Mars and Jupiter, there appears to be a fairly large open area. It's not empty, though. It's filled with tons of

SOLAR WINDS FROM THE SUN EXTEND OUT PAST NEPTUNE.

asteroids. That's why it's called the asteroid belt. Looking closer, there appears to be enough room for another planet. So why didn't one form? Well, there is a dwarf planet, Ceres, there. But no "true" planet. Perhaps when the solar system was forming, not enough clumps came together there to form a "true" planet. Some scientists believe that because Jupiter is so large, it disrupted the formation of a nearby planet.

Beyond Neptune the space is filled with clumps of ice and dirt. Scientists

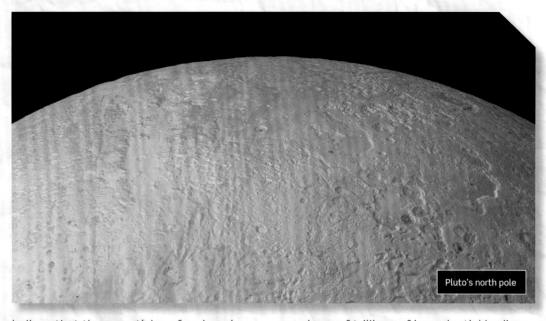

Pluto's north pole

believe that those particles of rock and gases were too far from the sun and too sparsely distributed to heat up and clump together to form large planets. So this area, called the Kuiper (KY-per) belt, has dwarf planets, sometimes called plutoids, instead. In fact, Pluto, the former planet, is now categorized as one of these. Some are large objects, but not big enough to have enough gravity to clear out the area around them. Scientists think thousands of these small, icy objects like Pluto can be found in the Kuiper belt. Farther out from the Kuiper belt is the Oort cloud, which is made up of trillions of icy celestial bodies, or objects in orbit around the sun. A lot of comets, composed of ice, dirt, and rock, are from here. Many of the comets have very elliptical orbits. That means the comets spend most of their time in the Oort cloud, in the cold far reaches of the solar system. But when they swing by us, during their closest approach to the sun, their ices heat up and start to escape as gases, giving the comets their tails. The edge of the Oort cloud is considered to be the outer rim of our solar system.

TRY THIS

MAKE A SOLAR SYSTEM MODEL

Make a football-field-size model of the solar system, using an orange for the sun. Place it on one goal line. Using a scale of 1 foot (0.3 m) to 5 million miles (8 million km), Mercury would be about halfway between the two- and three-yard lines. Now determine the position of the other planets. (Note: Although the yard lines on a football field go from zero to 50 and back to zero, treat them as 100 continuous yard lines.)

AVERAGE DISTANCE FROM THE SUN

Mercury: 35 million miles (.387 AU)
Venus: 67 million miles (.722 AU)
Earth: 93 million miles (1 AU)
Mars: 142 million miles (1.52 AU)
Jupiter: 484 million miles (5.20 AU)
Saturn: 889 million miles (9.58 AU)
Uranus: 1.79 billion miles (19.2 AU)
Neptune: 2.8 billion miles (30.1 AU)

ROUND AND ROUND

The eight planets in our solar system orbit around the sun. Each planet travels in its own orbital path, which passes—but never comes into contact with—the sun or the other planets. The orbit of every planet is dependent upon the distance the planet is from the sun. Mercury has a very short orbit. It takes only 88 days to complete one trip around the sun. Earth, which is farther away, takes 1 year, or 365.25 days. But Jupiter takes almost 12 Earth years to orbit the sun, and Neptune needs almost 165 Earth years to complete its orbit! The farther the planet is from the sun, the longer its orbit takes.

As each planet revolves around the sun, it also rotates on its own axis. Earth takes 24 hours to complete an axis revolution, while Mercury takes about six Earth months to complete its rotation. Jupiter, the largest planet, rotates so rapidly it only takes just under 10 Earth hours. Venus is the slowest rotating planet—it requires more than 243 Earth days to complete just one rotation. That is one looong day!

All of the planets revolve counterclockwise around the sun, but they don't all rotate counterclockwise on their axes. Venus and Uranus are the only two planets that rotate clockwise.

> BECAUSE VENUS TAKES 243 EARTH DAYS TO ROTATE ONCE ON ITS AXIS AND ONLY 225 EARTH DAYS TO COMPLETE ONE ORBIT AROUND THE SUN, A DAY ON VENUS IS LONGER THAN A YEAR THERE!

The orbits and individual rotations of each planet create a cycle within the planet. For example, one rotation of the Earth is how we measure one day. One complete orbit around the sun is how we measure one year. It is much the same on other planets. Every planet has its own night/day cycle and yearly cycle.

TRY THIS

SPINNING EARTH

How does Earth move on its axis?

MATERIALS:
- A ball of modeling clay (to represent the Earth)
- A long toothpick (to represent the Earth's axis)

1. Take a toothpick and push it through the center of your ball of modeling clay so that just the ends of the toothpick poke through the ball.

2. Using your thumb and pointer finger, give the toothpick-ball a spin, like it's a top.

3. Watch how the top of the toothpick moves as the ball spins.

4. You should see the toothpick move in a circle. This is just how the Earth's axis spins.

5. Now try spinning it again. This time watch what happens to the ball of modeling clay.

6. You should see the ball wobble slightly as it spins.

7. This is exactly what the Earth does as it rotates on its axis. The small wobbles are not noticeable to us here on Earth. The reason it wobbles is that the Earth is not perfectly round and its weight is not perfectly distributed across the axis.

chapter 2

DWARF PLANETS,
METEORS, ASTEROIDS,
AND COMETS

1 EMERGENCY! NEW HORIZONS SPACE PROBE IS FREEZING UP! WE NEED YOU TO FIX IT RIGHT AWAY.

2

5 LET'S HOOK UP THE LASER. WE NEED TO MELT THIS ICE RIGHT AWAY.

BRRR ... BETTER TURN UP THE HEAT IN HERE, TOO, ROVER. IT'S FREEZING.

BUT THAT'S NOT SURPRISING, SINCE PLUTO IS BETWEEN 30 AND 50 TIMES FARTHER FROM THE SUN THAN EARTH!

ZAP!

6

20

DWARF PLANETS,
METEORS, ASTEROIDS,
AND COMETS

Space is vast. While it might seem empty to us here on Earth, it's actually filled with thousands of objects. Dwarf planets, meteors, asteroids, comets, and farther away, around other stars, there are even other entire solar systems.

PLUTO GOT ITS NAME FROM AN 11-YEAR-OLD GIRL. SHE SUGGESTED THE NAME TO HER GRANDFATHER, WHO SENT IT TO THE LOWELL OBSERVATORY, THE PLACE PLUTO WAS FIRST DISCOVERED.

BIG, BUT NOT BIG ENOUGH

Pluto used to be called a planet. But in 2006 it was reclassified as a dwarf planet. Why? Because although it does orbit the sun, and has a nearly round shape, this dwarf planet cannot clear the neighborhood around it. That means that the space around Pluto can contain asteroids or other objects in its orbit that a planet's gravity would prevent.

There are five known dwarf planets in our solar system: Ceres, Pluto, Haumea, Makemake, and Eris. Only Ceres is found in the asteroid belt between Mars and Jupiter. The rest are found at the outer rim of the solar system, in or near the Kuiper belt. Dwarf planets can have moons and, in fact, a couple of them do. Pluto has five moons, Haumea has two, and Eris has one tiny moon. The other two do not have moons.

ME AND MY SHADOW

Pluto and its largest moon, Charon, are close. Really close. They orbit only 12,000 miles (19,312 km) apart. Some scientists have said that Charon and Pluto are a double-dwarf system since their orbits are so close to each other. Their orbits are called synchronous, meaning that they move together as they orbit. They only ever show the same side to each other. It's almost as if they were joined by an invisible tether.

MEET THE DWARF PLANETS

PLUTO: Located in the Kuiper belt, Pluto is at different times between 30 and 50 times farther from the sun than Earth is. Pluto is believed to be about 60 percent rock and 40 percent nitrogen, methane, carbon monoxide, and water ice. When Pluto is closer to the sun, the methane, carbon monoxide, and nitrogen sublimate—they heat up and turn into gas. As Pluto gets farther from the sun, they freeze again onto the surface. Pluto is the largest dwarf planet discovered so far. In 2015, NASA's New Horizons team sent a spacecraft to Pluto and the Kuiper belt. During the flyby, scientists gathered valuable information about Pluto's geology and atmosphere.

This photo shows Pluto's rough, icy surface. Pluto's surface is a mix of nitrogen, methane, carbon monoxide, and water ice.

WHAT IS A DWARF PLANET?

Dwarf planets have many of the same characteristics as main planets, with one significant difference. According to the International Astronomical Union (IAU), a dwarf planet is a celestial body that

A is in orbit around the sun,

B has enough mass that its gravity pulls it into a nearly round shape,

C has not cleared the neighborhood around its orbit, and

D is not a satellite (such as a moon) of a bigger planet.

The one part of this definition that makes Pluto a dwarf planet and not a "real" planet is that it can't clear its orbit.

This art shows Eris and its moon Dysnomia.

ERIS: Slightly smaller than Pluto, Eris takes 557 Earth years to orbit the sun. It is way, way out at the edge of the solar system. The planet is believed to have a rocky center like Pluto. It may have a very thin atmosphere, but it is hard to tell from this distance. Scientists think that the atmosphere may collapse into an icy film on the surface of the planet when it is far away from the sun. It is estimated that temperatures on the surface of Eris can be as cold as minus 405°F (-243°C). *Brrrrrr.*

CERES: Ceres is the only dwarf planet found in the asteroid belt between Mars and Jupiter. Many scientists believe that it may have once had the opportunity to become a planet, but its closeness to Jupiter's massive gravitational pull prevented that. Ceres has low density and has water ice underneath its rocky surface. The amount of water within Ceres may be greater than all of the freshwater on Earth. Some scientists think Ceres may have formed farther out in the Kuiper belt and then been flung into the asteroid belt when the giant planets were still finalizing their orbital positions.

This photo, taken by NASA's Dawn spacecraft, shows Occator crater as a bright spot on Ceres's surface.

HAUMEA: This odd-shaped dwarf planet is one of the fastest rotating objects in the entire solar system. It completes one whole rotation on its axis in just four hours! The fast speed may account for its egg-shaped appearance. Haumea is about the same size as Pluto and has two moons orbiting it. At such a great distance from the sun, it is believed to have a rocky core and an icy exterior.

This art shows Haumea and its moons Hi'iaka and Namaka.

HAUMEA IS THE THIRD-BRIGHTEST OBJECT IN THE KUIPER BELT. ON A NIGHT WITHOUT CLOUDS AND WITH A GOOD TELESCOPE, YOU CAN SEE HAUMEA IN THE NIGHT SKY EVEN THOUGH IT IS HUNDREDS OF MILLIONS OF MILES AWAY.

MAKEMAKE: Like Pluto and Haumea, Makemake is found in the Kuiper belt, beyond the orbit of Neptune. This remote dwarf planet is slightly smaller than Pluto and believed to be just as icy. Its surface may have pellets of methane. Methane is normally a gas on Earth, but because of the cold it probably turns into a solid on Makemake. This dwarf planet has a reddish-brown color when seen through a telescope. This might be from the tholins—carbon-bearing molecules that form from solar ultraviolet radiation.

This art shows what we think Makemake's surface looks like.

ASTEROIDS: WATCH OUT FOR FLOATING RUBBLE

You might think asteroids are just giant rocks floating around in space. You would be wrong. Scientists believe that asteroids are actually composed of tons of broken pieces of metal, rock, and ice. Think of it this way. You take a glass ball and smash it. It breaks

> EGG-SHAPED ASTEROID 2008 HJ IS ONLY 39 FEET (12 M) WIDE AND ABOUT 79 FEET (24 M) LONG, MAKING IT SMALLER THAN A BASKETBALL COURT. BUT IT IS THE FASTEST SPINNING OBJECT IN THE SOLAR SYSTEM. IT COMPLETES ONE ROTATION EVERY 42.7 SECONDS!

into hundreds or thousands of tiny pieces. Now try to re-assemble it. If you can manage to glue all the pieces back together, you may be able to re-form the original shape. Well, sort of. It would be hard to get all of the pieces back into just the right place. That is how an asteroid forms. Once the broken pieces are free, they float around until they are gravitationally attracted to a larger clump of pieces and then latch on. You could say that asteroids are the vacuum cleaners of space.

Asteroids are not quite big enough to be called dwarf planets, but not small enough to be overlooked. They have no atmosphere so they can't support life. While asteroids do orbit the sun, and their orbits are fairly stable, they are found mostly in the asteroid belt between Mars and Jupiter. There are millions of asteroids in the asteroid belt. Still, if you add up the mass of the asteroids in the solar system, it would be less than that of Earth.

It is thought that asteroids are extra pieces of rock left over from the formation of the solar system. They could have formed planets, but didn't. Most asteroids have not changed much in billions of years. Because of this, scientists believe that they can provide clues about the beginnings of our solar system and how it was made.

SCIENTIST PROFILE

MEENAKSHI WADHWA

Dr. Meenakshi Wadhwa wants to know how our solar system began and how it's changing. And to do that, she studies pieces of rocks. As the director for the Center for Meteorite Studies at Arizona State University, she studies meteorites—the bits of space rock (often from an asteroid or comet) that fall to Earth—Martian rocks, and moon rocks. By studying rocks from around the solar system, she can compare the metals they contain. That tells her a lot about when and where the rocks formed.

This photo of asteroid Itokawa was taken by the Japanese space agency (JAXA) spacecraft Hayabusa (shown as art added onto the photo).

NAME THAT CELESTIAL BODY

Deciding on a name for a newly discovered star, comet, or moon is not as easy as it sounds. There are rules for naming every kind of celestial body and all of the names are ultimately certified by the International Astronomical Union. Yes, there are people whose job is to sit around and debate how to name a new celestial body. Many planets have a theme. Pluto, for example, and all of its surrounding bodies have mythological names associated with the underworld: Charon, Kerberos, Nix, and Styx. Other dwarf planets are given names that relate to gods or figures of creation, such as Makemake and Haumea, which are both gods of creation and fertility. Objects surrounding Saturn are named after the Greco-Roman titans. Examples include Prometheus, Atlas, Calypso, and, of course, Titan. Minor planets and comets are also given specifically chosen names.

AN ARTIST'S CONCEPTION OF CERES (RIGHT), WHICH IS NAMED FOR THE ANCIENT ROMAN GODDESS OF AGRICULTURE (STATUE, ABOVE)

COMETS: DIRTY SNOWBALLS OF SPACE

Comets are icy objects that release gas or dust. Many scientists refer to them as dirty snowballs. If you've ever held a dirty snowball in your hand, you know what they mean. It's a tightly packed ball of snow with bits of dirt, mud, and rocks in it. (Definitely not nice for throwing in a snowball fight!) Comets also contain a bunch of gases—carbon dioxide, ammonia, and methane, to name a few. Basically, comets are another kind of leftover dregs— deposits—from the beginning of the solar system. They didn't become part of a planet, a dwarf planet, or even an asteroid. Instead, they hang out in the Oort cloud at the far edge of the solar system, slowly orbiting the sun just like all the other bodies in the solar system.

Every once in a while a comet will streak through the inner solar system. Some do that on a regular basis and some only once every century or so. When that happens, the ice on the comet heats up and is released as a gas cloud, or coma. The radiation of the sun combined with the speed of the comet push the coma slightly behind the core, making the comet appear to have a brightly lit tail. Sometimes these tails are visible from Earth without a telescope. It's easy to identify a comet because the tail always points away from the sun.

Occasionally the comet tail will leave a trail of meteors in its wake. These meteors can fall to Earth. The Perseid meteor shower that appears every year between August 9 and 13 is the result of the Earth passing by the Swift-Tuttle comet.

For many years scientists have wanted to study a comet up close. In 2014, the European Space Agency (ESA) successfully

This art shows comet Wild 2.

DUST MATTERS

From 1999 to 2006, NASA's Stardust mission was out to collect a very special kind of dust—comet dust—from comet Wild 2. Comet dust and interplanetary dust particles (IDPs) are small—but they could hold huge insights into the history of the solar system and the origins of life. In these particles, which are leftovers from solar system formation, stardust scientists found an amino acid also found in living organisms. This discovery supports one idea that some scientists have proposed: The building blocks of life could have formed far from Earth and ended up here due to a meteorite or comet collision! Next time you pull out your broom and dustpan, think about *that*.

METEOROIDS THAT ENTER EARTH'S ATMOSPHERE BURN UP TO BECOME METEORS, OR SHOOTING STARS.

landed a probe on comet 67P/Churyumov-Gerasimenko. Called the Rosetta comet mission, it is the first landing of a space probe on a moving comet. Scientists are thrilled with the images and information they have received from this study. It is taking their understanding of the composition, movement, and geography of a comet to a whole new level.

SCIENTIST PROFILE

CLAUDIA ALEXANDER

Dr. Claudia Alexander was a NASA project scientist who was a principal project manager in developing the 10-year Rosetta comet mission. She had a Ph.D. in plasma physics and understood how gases worked in space. Landing the space probe on the comet was a feat never before achieved and Dr. Alexander oversaw NASA's contribution to the European mission. Dr. Alexander worked at the Jet Propulsion Laboratory and began her work with NASA on the Galileo mission to Jupiter, which discovered more than 21 moons and studied the atmosphere of the planet.

OUR NIGHT SKY

Of course, when you look up into the night sky, most of what you see are stars. Stars are giant balls of extremely hot gases called plasma, which are held together by gravity. Our galaxy, the Milky Way, is filled with billions of stars, including our own sun. Most of the stars we see in the sky are trillions of miles away from us. And yet they glow brightly and seem so close to us because they give off their own light.

The amount of energy generated by the core of a star determines how strong the light is and also how long it will last. Some stars last for tens of millions of years, while others may last for only 100,000 years. Eventually, stars will use up all of their energy. At that point they die out or collapse completely upon themselves before exploding into a supernova.

We tend to recognize or name stars by the way that they appear in groups. Their shapes or patterns are called constellations. Ancient astronomers gave names to certain constellations that looked like figures or animals. A constellation called Ursa Minor means "Small Bear," for instance. Ursa Minor contains the North Star, one of the most recognized stars in all of the night sky.

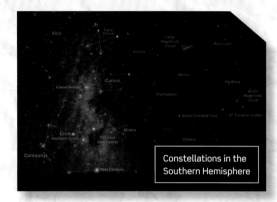

Constellations in the Southern Hemisphere

TRY THIS

MAKE YOUR OWN STAR VIEWER

MATERIALS:
- A star map
- Scissors
- A piece of black construction paper
- A thumbtack
- A piece of craft foam
- A metal brad
- A paper towel roll

1. Look online to print out a star map for your area and time of year. Cut it into a circle and glue it to the piece of black construction paper. Be sure the black circle is slightly bigger than the star map so that you can label the constellations.

2. Take the thumbtack and poke through all of the holes in the star map.

3. Turn the black paper over and label the constellations.

4. Cut a circle out of the craft foam big enough to fit around the paper towel roll and be sure to have a tab for it to be mounted in the center of the star map.

5. Use the metal brad to attach the craft foam spinner to the center of the star map.

6. Stick the paper towel roll into the open circle in the craft foam. You should be able to swing the paper towel roll around the star map, with the tab in the craft foam holding it centered.

7. Hold the star map up to the light and look through the paper towel roll. It should look like looking at stars in the night sky! Rotate the star map so that new constellations appear in your view.

URSA MAJOR, OR THE GREAT
BEAR. THIS CONSTELLATION ALSO
INCLUDES THE STAR PATTERN
KNOWN AS THE BIG DIPPER.

PLANETS

3
LOOK AT THAT. IT REALLY DOES LOOK LIKE IT'S GETTING SMALLER. WHAT DO YOU THINK, ROVER? CHECK YOUR DATA BANKS.
BEEP-BEEP
THE RED SPOT LOOKS LIKE IT'S ONLY A LITTLE OVER 10,000 MILES ACROSS. THE EARTH IS STILL SMALLER AT ABOUT 8,000 MILES, BUT THE SPOT IS DEFINITELY SMALLER THAN IT USED TO BE.
6
SET COURSE FOR SATURN, ROVER. THIS STORM WE HAVE TO SEE!
ZOOM!
WATCH OUT FOR THAT MOONLET, ROVER. THOSE TINY ASTEROID MOONS ARE EVERYWHERE IN SATURN'S OUTER RINGS.
7
BEEP!
STOP, ROVER. WE CAN GET SOME DATA HERE. WE'LL MAKE SATURN OUR LAB FOR THE NEXT FEW DAYS. TELL HOME BASE IF THEY WANT ME THEY CAN JUST GIVE ME A RING.

PLANETS

Why do scientists study *all* the planets? Why don't we just look at Earth alone? The rocks and terrain of each planet tell a story about how it was formed. Scientists use spacecraft, satellites, and robot-driven vehicles to explore other planets to try to piece together how our solar system was created. If we can understand that, then maybe we can learn more about how the Earth came to exist.

MEET MERCURY

Every one of the eight planets is different. They each have their own atmosphere, climate, and topography. The four inner planets are the ones closest to the sun, which means they are also the hottest. The sun emits its energy, or radiation, in the form of electromagnetic waves, spreading out in every direction. The planets closer to the sun receive a much higher amount of heat and radiation than those farther away. It's as if you were standing next to a fireplace. You get very hot if you stand close, but if you stand farther away, you can still feel toasty without getting overheated.

The heat each planet absorbs also depends upon the atmosphere of the planet. Mercury has an extremely thin atmosphere, which means its surface feels the full force of the sun's radiant heat. Daytime temperatures on Mercury can soar to a scorching 840°F (450°C). But since there is very little atmosphere to keep the heat in at night, the temperatures plunge to minus 275°F (-170°C). That's a one-day swing of more than 1100°F (620°C)! The lack of atmosphere gives Mercury another characteristic. Mercury is very rocky and full of craters, like the Earth's moon. Why so

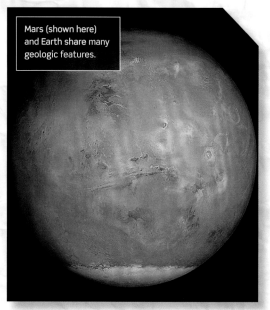

Mars (shown here) and Earth share many geologic features.

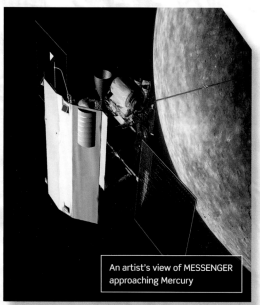

An artist's view of MESSENGER approaching Mercury

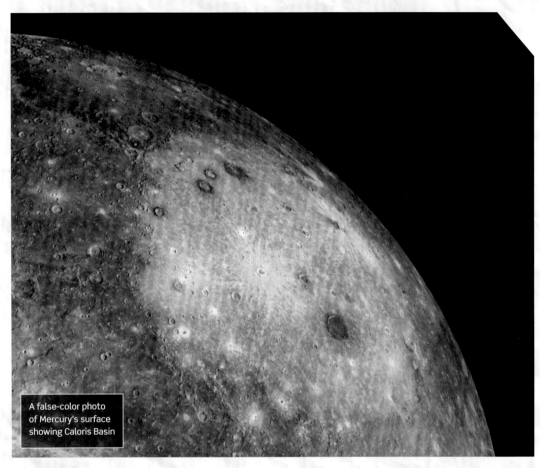

A false-color photo of Mercury's surface showing Caloris Basin

many craters? The surface is very old and there's almost no atmosphere to prevent meteors from slamming into the surface.

In 2012, NASA sent a probe called MESSENGER to orbit Mercury to record its geology. MESSENGER found an enormous crater measuring more than 960 miles (1,550 km) wide, which is believed to have been created more than four billion years ago by a strike from a massive asteroid. Scientists named the crater the Caloris Basin, and it's so huge that it could hold the entire state of Texas within its borders. It's even possible that another huge impact from a different asteroid could have con-tributed to the planet's slow spin. Mercury

takes almost 176 Earth days to spin once around its axis. It takes only 88 days to orbit the sun. Scientists believe that Mercury's rotation speed was originally similar to Earth's, but a strike from a huge asteroid slowed it down. The most unexpected result from the data gathered by the probe was the presence of ice in some of the craters around Mercury's north pole. Permanently shadowed by the crater rims, some of these craters haven't seen the sun for billions of years and have been trapping gas as ice. Finding water on a planet is significant since water is necessary for all life, and Mercury may have a record of the oldest water in the solar system.

VENUS AND MARS

Of the four inner planets, Venus, Earth, and Mars have gaseous atmospheres. Those atmospheres help protect their surfaces from the harsh rays of the sun. Venus has the densest atmosphere of all the inner

THE HOTTEST PLANET IS ACTUALLY VENUS, WHICH IS THE SECOND PLANET FROM THE SUN. THE REASON? MERCURY DOESN'T HAVE MUCH OF AN ATMOSPHERE, BUT VENUS'S VERY THICK GASEOUS ATMOSPHERE TRAPS THE SUN'S RADIATION, KEEPING THE ENTIRE PLANET AT A BALMY 875°F (468°C). SOMEONE TURN UP THE AIR CONDITIONING!

planets. It is mostly made up of carbon dioxide—yes, the gas we breathe out when

we exhale. There is also a little bit of nitrogen and clouds of toxic sulfuric acid thrown in. Not a great place for humans, for sure! The atmosphere acts like a huge thermal blanket, trapping the heat from the sun inside and letting temperatures rise even higher than on Mercury! This thick atmosphere prevents us from getting a good look at the surface, but scientists have conducted extensive radar imaging of the planet. Venus has similar topography to Earth: mountains, valleys, craters, plains, and even volcanoes and lava flows.

Mars has an extremely thin atmosphere. Its atmosphere is made of carbon dioxide, like

Oxia Palus region of Mars

This radar image shows Venus beneath the clouds. Red areas are high elevations, such as mountains, and blue areas are low elevations, such as valleys.

A DAY ON MARS

Ever wonder what it would be like to live on Mars? It would be very different from Earth, that's for sure. First of all, you would have to wear a space suit all the time. Without a magnetic field or much of an atmosphere to shield you from the sun's radiation, your skin would burn in a few minutes, and you would need your suit to give you oxygen to breathe. In the morning, you might see some frost on the rocks, left over from the high humidity (moisture in the air) at night. The daytime sky looks a bit orange, from all of the dust in the air. If it's a clear day, you may see some tiny, wispy clouds overhead or dust devils in the distance. But if one of the planet's big dust storms kicks up, hold on. It can last from days to months.

You might go exploring, because Mars has some beautiful places to visit: the polar ice caps, the tallest volcano in the solar system, and even a giant system of valleys that stretches miles (km) across the surface. But keep in mind, it's going to be much harder to walk or run on Mars because it has only 38 percent of Earth's gravity. You'd be better off leaping, jumping, or just driving around in your land rover. Still, the clear sky at night gives you an amazing view of the millions of stars overhead—a peaceful end to your glorious Martian day.

Scientists are developing new space suits that would let astronauts move around easily on Mars.

Venus's, but it is only 0.6 percent as thick as Earth's atmosphere. Since its atmosphere is more than 100 times thinner than Earth's it cannot trap and keep much of the sun's heat. The lack of this insulating blanket, and the fact that it is farther from the sun, makes it very cold, much colder than Earth. Temperatures on the surface of Mars can range from minus 195°F (-125°C) near its poles in winter to a much more comfortable 70°F (20°C) near the equator. Mars has large polar caps of water ice, like Earth.

Why is Mars called the "red planet"? Because its entire surface has a very thin layer of fine reddish iron oxide dust. It's kind of like baby powder, only it's rusty red, not white. Dust storms kick up on Mars and can cover the entire planet. They can last for months! That would make life challenging on Mars, at least near the surface. Beneath the dust is basalt rock, an igneous rock that comes from a volcano. This type of rock is similar to some types of rocks found on Earth, like on volcanoes in Iceland and Hawaii, and on volcanic vents on Earth's seafloor.

TRY THIS

FINDING FROST

1. How does Mars have frost if it has no water? It's all about the humidity, or moisture in the air.

2. Take a clean, dry jar and place the lid on it.

3. Now put it in a freezer for at least an hour.

4. Remove and observe. At room temperature, the air inside the jar was not saturated with moisture, but in the cold freezer the air could not hold as much water—it became saturated—and the water condensed and formed frost.

OUR HOME PLANET

Earth. It's where we live, work, and play. It's the one planet in our solar system that contains an excess of the most important material for life: water. Without water, there is no life as we know it. So how did our planet become the Earth we know and love?

Bam! A massive collision between the early version of the Earth and another Mars-size rock, now called Theia, is believed to have not only created our planet, but our moon as well. Debris from the collision clumped together and began to orbit Earth. Eventually, this clump of debris became our moon. Over time, the bits of planet that stayed together as our Earth cooled, which created a solid crust and allowed water to form.

The crust, while solid, is separated into different pieces, or plates, which can move independently based on the intense heat under it in Earth's next layer called the mantle. This movement is called plate tectonics, and is responsible for some of the geologic features we see on the surface of Earth.

TAKING A WALK ON JUPITER

It's not as easy as it sounds. Jupiter is made mostly of clouds and gas. In order to find a solid surface to stand on, and not sink through, you would have to go through many layers of gases to get to the core. Assuming you survived the descent through the deadly hydrogen and helium gas, the layer of ammonia ice, the searing heat, and the winds of more than 328 feet per second (100 m/sec), you would enter a layer of liquid gas. Think steam in a hot tub, but deadly. After wading through the liquid you would have to swim through a layer of highly metallic hydrogen that hosts the strongest magnetic field in the solar system, besides the sun's. Finally, you would hit the core, a relatively solid surface that might feel like a rocky sand dune. There you would feel atmospheric pressures of about 40,000 times greater than Earth's and temperatures of more than 63,000°F (35,000°C).

GIANT JUPITER

The four outer planets are much farther away from the sun—out past Mars and the asteroid belt. The outer planets are much larger than the inner planets and all have very dense atmospheres. It is assumed that there must be a rocky core somewhere in Jupiter, but it is under the weight of thousands of Earth atmospheres. The four outer planets are often called the gas giants. Why gas giants? These planets are made up mostly of gases, like helium and hydrogen.

Unlike the inner planets, they have small, rocky cores.

The largest of the gas giants is Jupiter, and sometimes these four outer planets are called Jovian planets, after it. Jupiter is so big that it

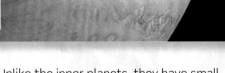

THE RED SPOT ON JUPITER IS ACTUALLY A HURRICANE-LIKE STORM THAT HAS BEEN GOING ON FOR MORE THAN 400 YEARS.

would take 11 Earths to stretch across its center. Jupiter has more than 50 moons orbiting it, some of which are the size of small planets.

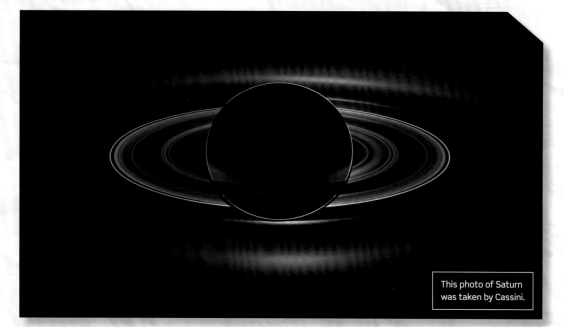

This photo of Saturn was taken by Cassini.

RING AROUND THE PLANET

Saturn, the sixth planet from the sun, is a lot like Jupiter, only smaller. It would take nine Earths to fit across its middle. The most noticeable thing about Saturn is its rings. While all of the gas giants have rings,

> IF YOU USED YOUR CAR, IT WOULD TAKE YOU MORE THAN A WEEK TO DRIVE ACROSS SOME OF SATURN'S RINGS.

Saturn's rings are the largest and brightest. They are made of bits of ice and rock. Some of these pieces are as small as a speck of sand; others are as big as a two-story house! How did they get there? Scientists believe that the rings might be pulverized fragments of asteroids that had hit the planet and then broke up in the atmosphere. The gravity from Saturn pulled them into orbit, which created the rings. Some of the rings are bits of ice and gas that are being ejected in plumes from Saturn's moon Enceladus.

The rings are not stationary. They move constantly, some of them swirling around Saturn at tens of thousands of miles an hour (km/h). Even though each main ring can be composed of many tiny ringlets, or smaller rings, they are all relatively thin. It's like a huge piece of tissue paper that's completely unfolded. The best information we have about the rings of Saturn comes from NASA's Cassini spacecraft, which was launched in 1997 and took seven years to reach Saturn. In 2004 it began sending back data and the most amazing pictures of Saturn and its rings.

SISTER PLANETS

The last two gas giants are Uranus and Neptune. They are sometimes called sister planets because they are so similar. They both have rocky inner cores like Jupiter and Saturn, but their outer cores are mostly composed of icy water and ammonia (a very strong-smelling liquid that is often used to clean things, like in your house). Their atmospheres consist of helium, hydrogen, and methane gases. And their outermost atmospheres are simply a line of thin, wispy, cloud tops.

Uranus's axis is tilted on its side. The planet also rotates backward—like Venus, it rotates clockwise. Uranus takes more than 84 years to travel around the sun, but it takes only 17 Earth hours to complete one rotation.

Neptune is one of the windiest and most dynamic of all the planets. Neptune emits, or gives off, 2.7 times more energy than it receives from the sun. Scientists believe this has to do with the extremely strong magnetic current produced within the planet. The magnetic field is tilted 47 degrees from the axis of the planet, which makes for dramatic changes in magnetic strength as the planet rotates. The big changes in the magnetic field may explain the huge winds in excess of 1,200 miles an hour (1,931 km/h) on the planet. Neptune also has auroras, like the northern lights seen on Earth, but they occur over vast distances and not just near Neptune's poles.

Uranus spins on its side.

Neptune

chapter 4

FROZEN WORLDS

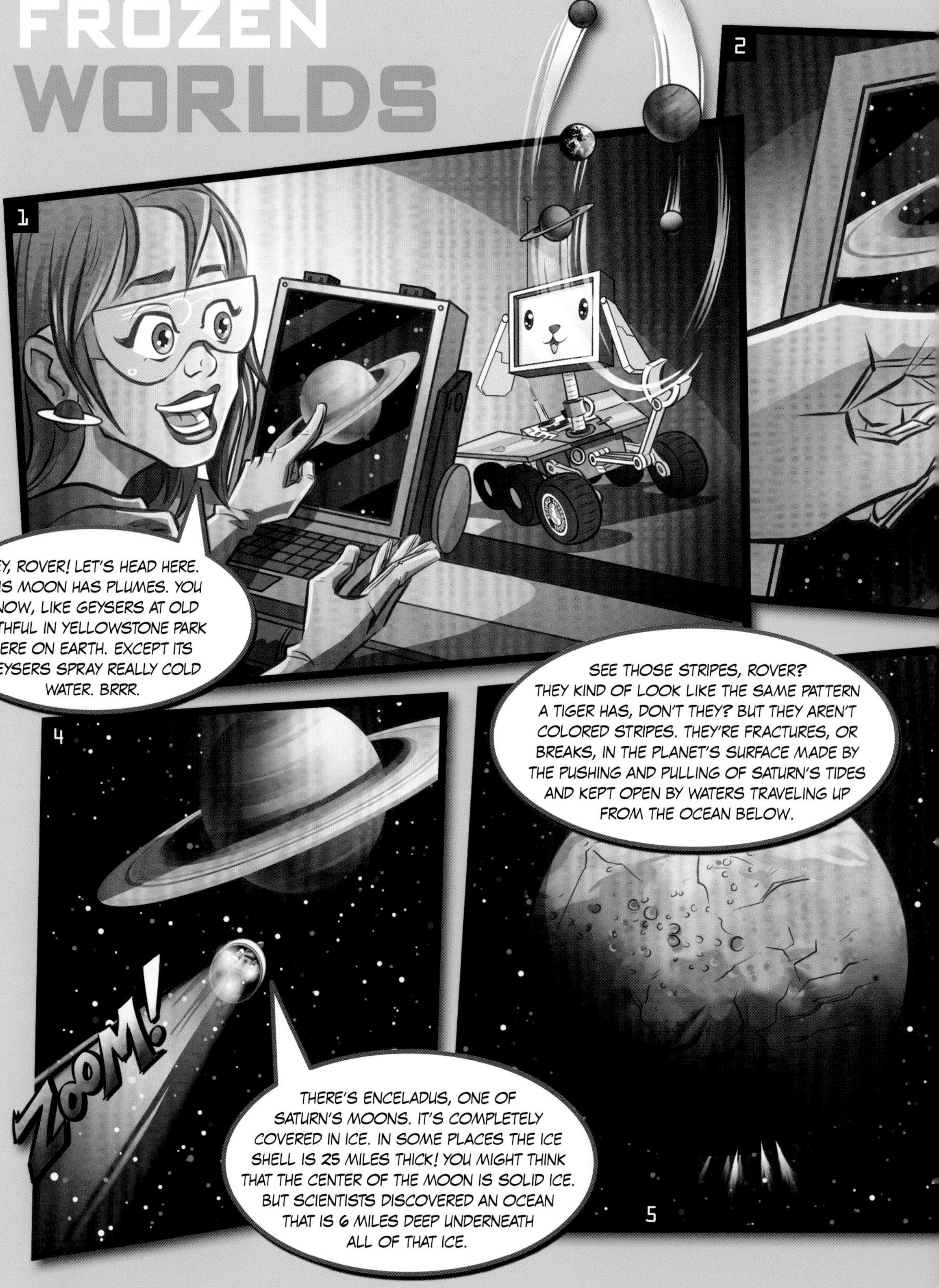

FROZEN WORLDS

Water. From microscopic organisms to a 380-foot (116-m) redwood tree, it's what all living things need to survive. The presence of water on Earth is what makes our planet livable for humans, too. It only makes sense that in our quest to explore the solar system, one of the main items we seek on other planets is water. For many years, we thought that Earth was the only planet to have liquid water. But by using spacecraft and probes to search the solar system, we discovered that there appears to be water on other planets and moons!

Two of Jupiter's moons, Europa and Ganymede, are believed to have liquid water beneath their icy crusts. Enceladus, one of Saturn's moons, has plumes of water shooting up into space. The two ice giants—Uranus and Neptune—certainly contain water, and even Mars is thought to have occasional water flowing across its landscape. In fact, the more we look through space, the more evidence we find that water might be there. With that reality, can the evidence of life be far behind? And what other surprises await us? The icy celestial bodies are a good place to look.

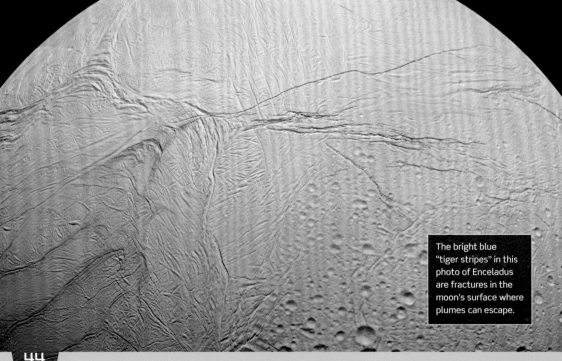

The bright blue "tiger stripes" in this photo of Enceladus are fractures in the moon's surface where plumes can escape.

ICY MOONS

Scientists once thought that Earth was the only celestial body to have active plate tectonics. Plate tectonics is the idea that the rocks that form the solid surface of Earth sit on different pieces of crust that "float" on top of Earth's mantle. Earth's mantle is hot, so hot that the mantle rocks deform like putty. As the heat churns the mantle, it creates convection currents, which can shift the plates in the crust and make them move.

But scientists have recently looked closely at the gas giants' moons. Evidence of a kind of plate tectonics has been found on Europa and Ganymede. Such evidence has also been found on Enceladus. Their icy crusts appear to be broken into large sections that hide huge oceans underneath. Scientists theorize that the icy oceans act like the mantle of the Earth, shifting the frozen crust on top and creating geologic features such as icy plumes of water in the process.

On Earth, the Alps were formed by plate tectonics.

TRY THIS

CREATE CONVECTION CURRENTS

1. Have an adult conduct this activity while you make observations.

2. Take the temperature of the soup. It should be cold.

3. Turn the burner on so the soup begins to heat up.

4. After several minutes, put the thermometer into the soup. Measure the temperature of the bottom of the soup—but don't let the thermometer touch the bottom of the pan. Now measure the top of the soup. The two temperatures should be slightly different.

5. Stir the soup and take the temperature again. What happened? As the warm soup was mixed with the cold soup, the temperature at the surface went up.

6. Wait a few minutes more. Take the temperature again of the bottom then the top. Their temperatures should be getting closer to each other. That is the convection current moving.

Now imagine this taking place deep within the Earth's mantle, below the crust. These convection currents can make the crustal plates move and shift as heat is transferred from the center of the Earth outward. You may notice this in the vegetables or noodles in the soup moving up and down as temperature changes.

MATERIALS:
- An adult to help
- A can of soup
- A pot or pan
- A stove
- A cooking thermometer

ENCELADUS'S PLUMAGE

Enceladus is the sixth largest moon of Saturn and may be one of the most promising places for finding life. Its crust is made of a thick shield of ice, but it hides a huge ocean of icy liquid water underneath. Plumes of icy water that shoot into the sky provide evidence for this hidden ocean. NASA's spacecraft Cassini witnessed several sprays coming from fractures in the planet near its southern pole.

The water vapor, salt, and organic particles

> ENCELADUS IS ONLY ABOUT 1/25 THE SIZE OF THE EARTH AND 1/6 THE SIZE OF OUR MOON. IF THE MOON WERE A SOCCER BALL, ENCELADUS WOULD BE ABOUT THE SIZE OF A **TABLE TENNIS BALL.**

indicate the presence of a global saltwater ocean that may be about the size of Lake Superior—the largest lake in North America. The ocean on Enceladus is probably much deeper than Lake Superior, perhaps more than six miles (9.7 km) deep. The icy water geysers may be similar to Old Faithful, the geyser in Yellowstone National Park here on Earth. One key difference seems to be that the geysers on Enceladus are continuous. It is believed that Saturn's gravitational forces create a sort of tidal push and pull on the cracks in the ice plates. This stretching and

Old Faithful, Earth

CRYOVOLCANOES

When you think of volcanoes, you probably think of hot, flowing lava. But not all volcanoes are hot. One of Saturn's moons, named Titan, has a volcano that may spew ice. Called a cryovolcano, this type of icy volcano shoots ice, water, and hydrocarbon into the air. While the intensely hot volcanoes on Earth can destroy life, the icy volcanoes in space might actually be a good place for life to start. The eruptions may be a way to mix the minerals from under the surface with those in the atmosphere.

contracting force shoots the water in between the cracks into the atmosphere.

The discovery of this amount of liquid water on a moon with tectonics similar to Earth's is pretty amazing. The ocean may rest upon a rocky bottom where all kinds of complex chemical reactions may be possible—including, perhaps, the kind that led to the rise of life on Earth.

MEET EUROPA

Europa is one of the larger moons orbiting Jupiter. It may also have a form of plate tectonics. The "plates" are sheets of ice more than 20 miles (32 km) thick that float on top of a liquid ocean. What's in the ocean? No one knows for sure. In the future, scientists hope to send a probe that can drill down deep beneath the sheets of ice to find out. Perhaps there are microorganisms—life!—inside its icy depths.

But if a spacecraft has not actually landed on the surface of Europa, how can we be sure there is water? First, data from a magnetometer suggests there's a fluid like water beneath Europa's surface, rather than a totally solid interior. Second, scientists have been studying the images of Europa's surface. It is a complex surface, full of light and dark patches, ridges, and troughs or long narrow openings in its outer crust. Parts of the crust even appear to have been rotated slightly, kind of like a puzzle piece that doesn't quite fit into place. Upon close inspection, the

THIS ART SHOWS A
GEYSER ON EUROPA.

This photo of Europa shows dark brown rocky areas and lighter icy areas.

surface is crisscrossed with bands that may have once been ridges or mountains that let out liquid materials from a deep ocean. These bands show evidence of a process like seafloor spreading on Earth, a process that is associated with plate tectonics.

Seafloor spreading on Europa might happen when two plates of ice move apart and the icy water from below moves up to fill in the empty space. This water freezes and becomes part of the surface, creating new crust. By measuring the density and magnetic field around Europa, scientists can figure out what is inside. They believe it has a metallic core, rocky mantle (or middle), liquid layer, and a thin, solid crust. The comparison to the Earth is a good one, except of course Earth's surface is much warmer than Europa's minus 260°F (-160°C).

TRY THIS

WANT TO KNOW HOW PLATE TECTONICS WORK?

MATERIALS:
- A piece of waxed paper
- Frosting or peanut butter
- Two graham crackers

1. Cut off a large sheet of waxed paper.

2. Cover it with a layer of frosting or peanut butter.

3. Take the two graham crackers and place them side by side. Do not leave a space in between.

4. Slowly pull them apart. You should see the frosting or peanut butter come up slightly in the space. That is like seafloor spreading.

5. Now remove one of the crackers and wet it slightly. Put it back on the layer of frosting or peanut butter.

6. Push the two graham crackers together hard. Does one lift up and create a sort of mountain? That is similar to how mountains are formed from the collision of two plates.

IT'S ALL ABOUT RECYCLING

Plate tectonics is a way for the Earth to recycle its old crust into new crust. As the plates push together, the heavier, denser plate goes below the lighter one and is absorbed back into the mantle. The same thing happens on Europa, except instead of descending into hot mantle rock, the warmer layer of ice below Europa's surface absorbs the descending old thick outer crust.

HOW DOES WATER GET THERE IN THE FIRST PLACE?

Vroom! Comets streak through the solar system, speeding toward a planet, their tails full of water ice trailing behind them. *Boom!* They crash into the surface. All at once, the water from their tails and the ice inside is released onto whatever they crashed into. Scientists believe that this is one way that many planets and moons may have gotten their water.

EROSION AND WEATHERING

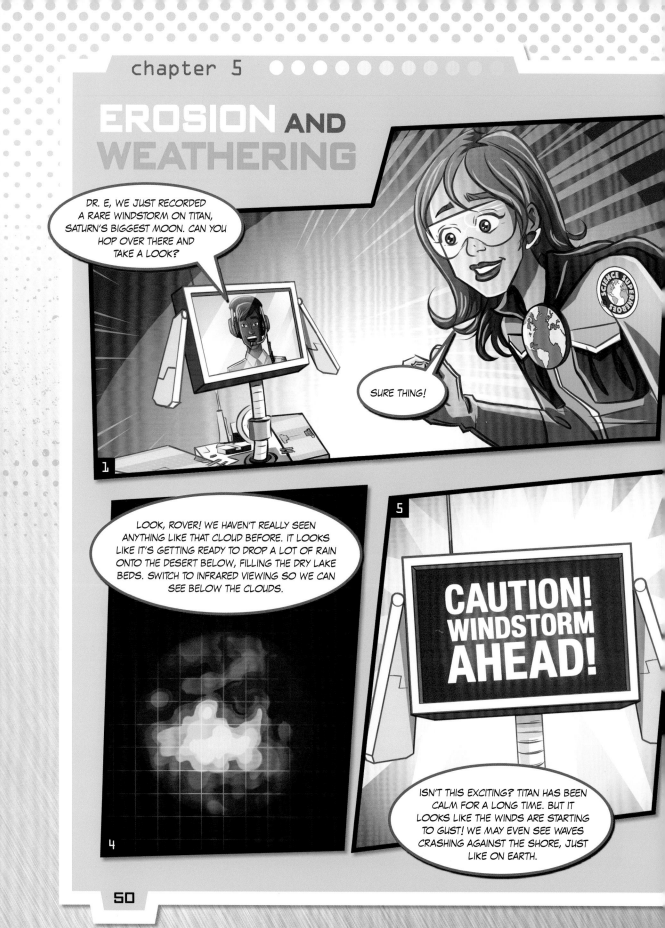

CHECK OUT THOSE CLOUDS, ROVER. YOU CAN SEE THEM FROM UP HERE. LOOKS LIKE A BIG STORM IS BREWING.

BEEP!

WHAT'S THAT? NO, ROVER. TITAN DOESN'T HAVE RAIN WATER SHOWERS LIKE WE DO ON EARTH. TITAN'S SHOWERS ARE MADE OF LIQUID METHANE. YOU KNOW HOW THE EARTH HAS A WATER CYCLE? WELL, TITAN HAS THE SAME TYPE OF CYCLE, EXCEPT IT'S WITH LIQUID METHANE.

WIND CREATES EROSION, MOVING THE DUNES AND CHANGING HOW THE SURFACE OF THE MOON LOOKS FROM ABOVE.

LOOK OVER THERE, ROVER! SEE THAT? THE DUNES ARE MOVING! WE HAVEN'T SEEN THAT IN 10 YEARS! THIS STORM IS HUGE! IT'S WEATHER IN ACTION!

WOOOOSH!

WOOOOSH!

EROSION
AND WEATHERING

Landforms on Earth and other worlds are created by plates crashing into each other, molten or icy lava flowing to the surface, and impacts with other celestial bodies. But once created, do these geologic

THE GRAND CANYON IN THE UNITED STATES IS THE RESULT OF CONSTANT WATER EROSION BY THE COLORADO RIVER OVER MILLIONS OF YEARS. IN FACT, EROSION IS STILL HAPPENING THERE TODAY!

structures stand forever? No! Eventually, over millions of years, everything breaks down. It's the cycle of matter. As the plates shift on Earth, pieces of the crust break off, slide under other slabs of crust and are turned into molten magma (liquid rock). A type of recycling process takes place above the surface of the Earth, too. It's called erosion and weathering.

EROSION UP CLOSE

Erosion happens to every landform you can think of, even the continents themselves. Mountains become hills, hills turn into valleys, and huge boulders become pebbles. It is a never-ending process. Erosion is caused primarily by wind or water. As wind blows across a mountain, it picks up tiny bits of dust or dirt and carries them away. That is erosion. If you imagine that happening hundreds of times a day over millions of years, you can see how a mountain would shrink.

Erosion with water occurs in much the same way. Water flows down a mountain while bits of dirt, rock, and mud from the sides and bottom of the stream are carried along with the water. When the clump of debris, known as sediment, gets big enough, it falls out of the water and ends up either at the bottom of the stream or perhaps at the point where the stream empties into a lake or river.

The Colorado River wears away rock in the Grand Canyon.

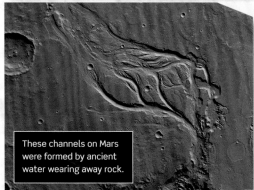

These channels on Mars were formed by ancient water wearing away rock.

LOOK OUT BELOW!

On Earth, gravity is an overwhelming force, and one that causes erosion to always occur in a downhill direction. Think about it. If a gust of wind knocks a rock off the top of a cliff, where will it fall? To the ground, of course. That's erosion. Eventually, if the rock sits there long enough the wind and rain break it down further and turn it back into dust. That's erosion, too. Seems simple, doesn't it? It is.

This stone formation in Bolivia's Siloli Desert was caused by erosion.

TRY THIS

EROSION IN ACTION

Build your own mountain outside. Collect a big pile of dirt, rocks, and sand. Mold it into a mountain and pack it tightly together. Measure it at the highest peak. Take a picture of it. Over the next three weeks check the height and take a picture daily. Note the weather that occurred each day. Was it sunny, windy, rainy? At the end of the three weeks, make a chart of the heights of your mountain, and then graph it. You should see that the mountain's height went down as nature carried pieces away.

PHYSICAL OR CHEMICAL

Weathering, the wearing down of materials, takes place in two different forms. The first is called physical weathering. This is when rocks are broken down without any change in their chemical makeup. It's like when one rock hits another, smashing it into pieces. The bits of rock just experienced physical weathering.

Freezing and thawing of rocks can also be a form of physical weathering. As the water between the rocks freezes, it expands, breaking the rock apart. When the ice thaws, the pieces of the rock fall away, leaving smaller rocks.

The thawing ice, now water, penetrates the rock even farther, getting into its tiny crevices. As the water freezes yet again, the rock cracks some more. This process is repeated over and over for millions of years.

The second form of weathering is called chemical weathering. This happens when

After months of driving the Spirit rover, looking for evidence of ancient water, Dr. Ehlmann and colleagues discovered the first evidence for significant ancient water in this gnarly rock with little "nuggets" on top of stalks. Measurements showed the rock had been chemically weathered by water to form soft minerals then physically eroded. Dr. Ehlmann and her colleagues were so excited by this find, they nicknamed the rock "Pot of Gold."

chemical reactions break down rocks. Oxygen, carbon dioxide, and water combine with the minerals in the rocks and create new substances. Sometimes these new substances

VENUS'S ROCKY SECRETS

Venus is a planet almost totally shrouded in clouds. The heavy cloud cover makes it impossible to see the surface from an orbiting satellite or spacecraft. But in 1975, a Russian spacecraft was able to land on the surface and send back some amazing photos. The hard surface is littered with rocks of all sizes. Boulders, slabs, and pebbles are crisscrossed and randomly strewn across the entire area. Is that significant? Scientists think so. They see evidence of cycles that we have here on Earth: layering, fracturing, and even chemical and physical weathering. This tells them that some of the same processes on Earth and Mars are also present on Venus. Well, likely without the water.

Lavinia Planitia region of Venus

Badlands, Utah

are softer and cause the rock to break apart. Or the new substances are more easily washed away by wind or rain, taking bits of the rock with them.

Over millions of years, weathering and erosion can shape and change mountains, valleys, hills, and lakes on planets or moons.

They may break down a mountain in one area, but build up the sides of a valley in another. By studying a world's geologic features and then determining how the weathering and erosion there took place, scientists can learn how planetary worlds were formed, and also how they continue to change.

TRY THIS

CANDY WEATHERING

1. Place one candy in each glass.

2. Fill half of one glass with water.

3. Fill half of one glass with soda.

4. Leave the last glass empty.

MATERIALS:
- Three candy-coated chocolate candies, each a different color
- Three small, clear glasses
- Water
- Clear soda

Observe what happens to the candies over a period of four days. Make daily observations about any changes to the size, shape, or color of the candies and also the color of the water. At the end, note which candy weathered the most. Do you think it was chemical or physical weathering? (Hint: The bubbles in soda are caused by carbon dioxide.)

TITAN'S SAND DUNES

Got sand? Titan, Saturn's largest moon, does. The dunes there look like the sand dunes you would find on Earth. The thing is, they are made of different materials. While the sands of Earth are made of broken-down bits of rock and minerals called silicates, the sand dunes of Titan are composed of grains containing hydrogen and carbon.

> BECAUSE OF TITAN'S DENSE ATMOSPHERE AND LOW GRAVITY, YOU COULD PROBABLY FLY ABOVE ITS SURFACE SIMPLY BY STRAPPING A PAIR OF WINGS TO YOUR ARMS AND FLAPPING THEM.

The dunes of Titan are enormous—0.6 to 1.2 miles (1 to 2 km) wide and as high as 328 feet (100 m) in some places. That's as tall as a 30-story building! The dunes cover almost 13 percent of the moon, and stretch over a distance of 38 million square miles (100 million square km), which is about the size of Canada.

How did these huge dune fields form? On Earth, fast winds blowing across the sand whip particles into high dunes in a desert. Scientists were thinking that the same process would be at work on Titan. However, they noticed that the speeds they had estimated for the winds on Titan were 50 percent lower than they should be in order to move that amount of sand. To figure out how Titan could produce the sand dunes, Dr. Devon Burr of the University of Tennessee–Knoxville used an old wind tunnel at NASA to re-create the atmospheric conditions on Titan. Taking into account the lower gravity and density of the sand on Titan, her

Dr. Devon Burr and her team used this wind tunnel setup to re-create possible atmospheric conditions on Titan.

The ESA's Huygens probe took these photos of Titan's dunes as it landed on the moon's surface.

A Cassini orbiter radar image of the dunes on Titan

These sand dunes in Namibia, Africa, are the closest examples to Titan's dunes on Earth.

team had to use 24 different substances to make the sand. The mixture they ended up with weighed less than coffee grounds and included particles such as hollow glass spheres and walnut shells.

In the end, the scientists were able to determine that to move the sand particles, a wind

IN 2004, THE CASSINI-HUYGENS SPACECRAFT TRAVELED TO SATURN. IT SENT BACK NEVER BEFORE SEEN PHOTOS OF ITS SURFACE, MOONS, AND RINGS.

of 3.2 miles an hour (5.1 km/h) was needed. This was greater than their previous estimations. But is it accurate? No one knows for sure, at least not until a spacecraft can enter Titan's atmosphere and test out this theory. The significance of this finding is

that scientists here on Earth were able to mimic the environment on another object in the solar system, millions of miles away, and apply knowledge they have about how Earth works to potentially solve a mystery.

SCIENTIST PROFILE

DEVON BURR

Planetary geomorphology may sound complicated, but simply, it's the science of how planetary processes (like weathering and erosion) shape landforms. And Dr. Devon Burr is fascinated with it. On Mars, her research has focused on looking at flood channels, exploring the movement and deposit of sediment by ice, and mapping pingos (mounds of ice covered by a layer of soil). On Titan, she explores atmospheric conditions that could lead to possible rivers of liquid methane and to the sand dunes. To study these distant land features, Dr. Burr looks to Earth to find similar landforms, from the pingos of Alaska and Canada to the flood channels of Iceland.

NOT ONE DROP

A planet's atmosphere has a lot to do with whether liquid can exist there. If you could take a cup of water to the surface of Mars, the water would vaporize before you could drink it. Why? Mars's atmosphere is so thin that liquid water can't exist for very long. And yet, there is evidence on the surface that water was once present. Dried-up valleys, sedimentary deposits, and grooves that appear to have been worn through by old floodplains are clearly visible. So where did the water go?

Scientists believe that most of Mars's atmosphere was blown away by solar winds. Solar winds are streams of energized particles that flow outward from the sun, traveling at speeds of 895 to 1,790 miles an hour (1,440 to 2,880 km/h). The solar winds stripped away hydrogen and oxygen atoms from water vapor in the Mars atmosphere. Over time, this dried out the planet.

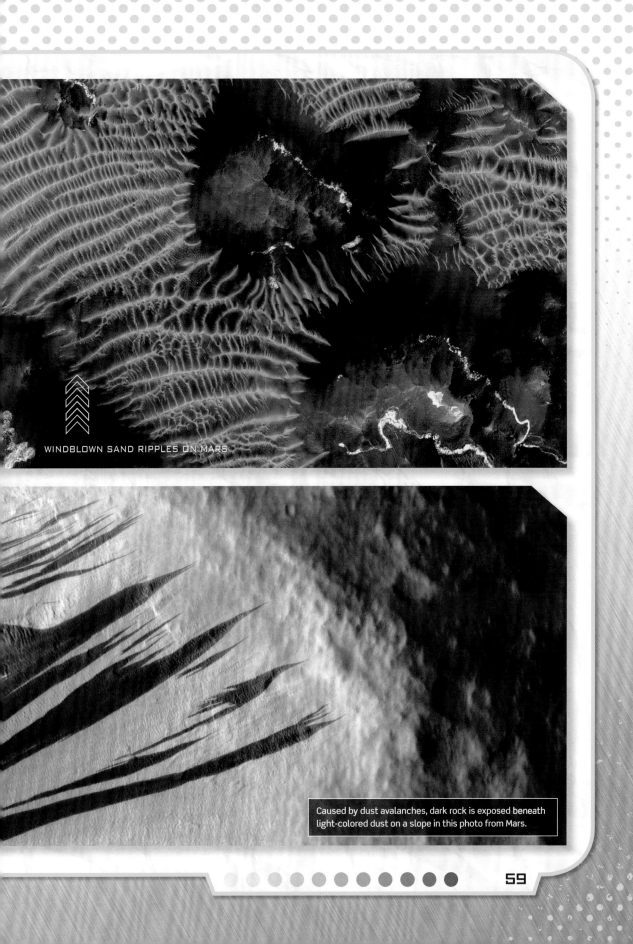

WINDBLOWN SAND RIPPLES ON MARS

Caused by dust avalanches, dark rock is exposed beneath light-colored dust on a slope in this photo from Mars.

VOLCANO WORLDS

VOLCANO WORLDS

The shifting tectonic plates beneath your feet cause changes in geology. On Earth, volcanoes frequently form when either two plates collide and one slips below the other, or when two plates move apart and create a gap. Other volcanoes, like the ones in the Hawaiian Islands, are caused by hot spots, areas where hot magma from the mantle, or subsurface, rises to the surface. The magma builds up in that area, creating a volcano. When the tectonic plate above it moves, the hot spot remains in the same area. As the plate moves, the hot spot creates a string of volcanoes over time. Hot spot, or plume, volcanism is likely very similar to the volcanic processes on other planets.

EARTH'S RING OF FIRE

A 25,000-mile (40,234-km)-long horseshoe-shaped area around the Pacific Ocean is the most dynamic place on the Earth. Known as the Ring of Fire, roughly 90 percent of all earthquakes and more than 75 percent of all volcanic activity occur at this location. But why does all of this energy happen here? It is due to shifting tectonic plates in the area. Seven different plates surround the Pacific plate. As the Pacific plate moves, it collides with other plates in the area. The collision of two massive plates of the Earth's crust can cause one to be shoved under the other (subduction) or to be pushed together to create mountains (a convergent boundary). A third shifting happens when two plates move away from each other and new magma comes up (a divergent boundary). All of these processes can result in earthquakes, tsunamis, or even the formation of volcanoes. This place is rockin'!

TYPES OF VOLCANOES

COMPOSITE VOLCANOES are cone-shaped. They have high walls and can stand more than 8,000 feet (2,440 m) tall. *Boom!* They can explode bits of ash, lava, rocks, and dust high into the air. The steaming hot lava then flows down the sides of the walls, burning everything in its path.

SHIELD VOLCANOES have low, sloping sides, and their eruptions are not explosive. The lava flows smoothly but quickly out the top and down the volcano in a seemingly endless supply.

CINDER CONE VOLCANOES are recognized by smaller, more rounded cones with a crater at the top. They have explosive eruptions, but they are mostly made of cinders, tiny pieces of gas-rich melted lava or bits of rock.

So how does a volcano work? When the Kilauea volcano erupts in Hawaii, the magma makes its way to the surface. A column of lighter, hotter magma within the mantle rises to the surface because it is less dense and because it can have tiny air bubbles. It's like a balloon of gases under the surface that expands. The gases get hotter and

THERE ARE MORE THAN 500 VOLCANOES ON THE EARTH'S SURFACE. MOST OF THEM ARE IN THE RING OF FIRE, AN AREA AROUND THE PACIFIC OCEAN.

hotter and the pressure rises until ... pop! The magma plume pushes through Earth's crust and hot lava—as the magma is then called—cascades down the sides of the volcano.

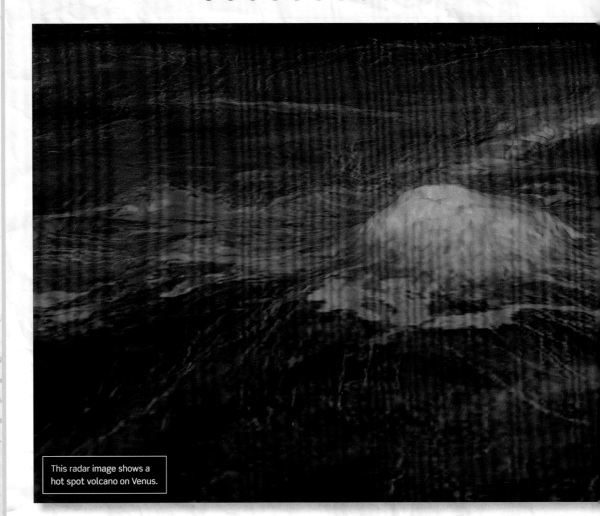

This radar image shows a hot spot volcano on Venus.

VOLCANIC VENUS

Earth is not the only planet with volcanic activity. Venus is practically Earth's twin. They are similar in size and shape and are fairly close neighbors in our vast solar system. Venus has hundreds of volcanoes. The question scientists are asking is—are the volcanoes still active? It's hard to tell from studies conducted by two different orbiters. Hot spots, or areas of heat under the surface, have been observed on the planet. These might indicate active volcanoes, but no lava has been found. The one thing scientists do know is that the level of sulfur dioxide—a gas released during an eruption—has increased over time in Venus's atmosphere. This might be because the volcanoes on Venus are actively erupting. Or not. The problem is that Venus has a super-rotating atmosphere that whips around the planet in only four Earth days. That mixes up all the gases and spreads them out across the sky, making it difficult to see their sources. Will the mystery of Venus's volcanoes ever be solved? Perhaps one day. NASA is developing plans to send another orbiter that would better see beneath the clouds. NASA might also send a lander robot to collect gases in the atmosphere and conduct measurements on the ground. This could only happen for a few

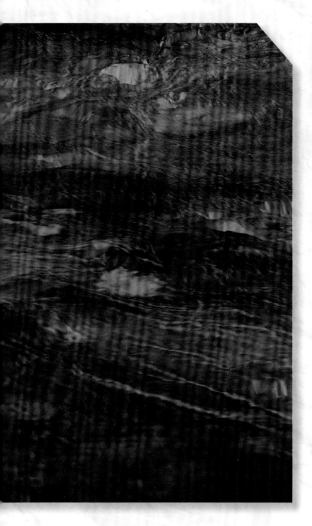

This photo shows an ongoing eruption on Io.

active because it is caught in the middle of a gravitational pull—from Jupiter on one side and the large moons, Europa, Ganymede, and Callisto, on the other. This puts enormous pushing and pulling pressure on Io as it navigates between all of these celestial bodies. Imagine you are walking two dogs on separate leashes and they both want to go in different directions. What happens? You get pulled first one way and then another. So you pull back both to get them closer to you. All of these actions are the same forces Io experiences.

Io "stretches" one way and then the other as it's pulled by the different gravitational fields. The result of these forces is heat. As the gravitational fields pull on the planet, its thin crust cracks and breaks and the molten lava underneath gushes to the surface. The pressure can cause huge and spontaneous geysers of lava to burst forth into the atmosphere. Scientists believe the volcanic activity on Io might hint at how Earth formed billions of years ago.

hours, though, before the robot fails due to high heat. At the surface of Venus, the temperatures are hot enough to melt lead. Now that's HOT!

ERUPTING Io

Jupiter's moon Io has the most active volcanoes of any object in our solar system. Io has an energetic environment. It has hundreds of volcanoes, lava flows, lava lakes, and even lava fountains, which erupt more than 250 miles (402 km) high. Why is Io so active? Does it have plate tectonics? Actually, no. Io's crust is not formed from different plates. It is so volcanically

Io WAS FIRST DISCOVERED BY GALILEO GALILEI IN 1610.

MASSIVE MARS VOLCANOES

Mars has the largest volcanoes in the entire solar system. Olympus Mons is a volcano 16.7 miles (27 km) tall. That's more than three times the height of Mount Everest. Talk about gigantic! Olympus Mons, along with three other giant volcanoes, is located in a section of Mars called Tharsis Montes. The four volcanoes started forming billions of years ago, but may have been active as recently as 20 million years ago.

Volcanoes in the Tharsis Montes region are 10 to 100 times the size of any volcano found on Earth. Why are they so massive? Hot spots within the center of the planet have kept things toasty for quite some time. As they fire up, the volcanoes become active, spewing lava for long periods of time. Another reason may be because Mars's crust doesn't move and shift like Earth's crust. Instead of being made up of

PIECES OF MARS HAVE BEEN FOUND IN METEORITES THAT LANDED ON EARTH.

different plates, like on Earth, Mars's crust appears to be one giant plate, or maybe two plates at the most. Scientists won't know

ROSALY LOPES

Dr. Rosaly Lopes has discovered more volcanoes in space than any other person, including 71 on Io alone. She is fascinated by the fiery and icy systems she finds there and the dynamic effect they have on their environments. She is a highly respected planetary geologist and senior research scientist at NASA's Jet Propulsion Laboratory. In 2006, Dr. Lopes was listed in the *Guinness World Records* as the discoverer of the most active volcanoes anywhere.

for sure until they can land an instrument called a seismometer to probe the layers deep under Mars's surface. But even if there are plates on Mars, they move very, very slowly. With an enormous amount of lava coming from the molten subsurface, it just piles upon itself, creating tremendously tall volcanoes.

Olympus Mons

HOW WERE THE HAWAIIAN ISLANDS FORMED?

A hot spot deep within Earth's crust spewed huge amounts of magma. As the Pacific plate slowly moved over it, lava rose up through the plate, cooled, and was deposited on the seafloor. Eventually the accumulated lava broke the surface of the water and formed the chain of Hawaiian Islands. Each island in the chain was formed at a different time, with the oldest one, Kauai, at the northwest point. A new volcano, Loihi, is still in formation and can be found 18.6 miles (30 km) southeast of Kilauea.

LET'S EXPLORE

69

LET'S EXPLORE

Scientists study space to learn more about how the solar system developed and also how we came to exist. But how can they gather data from stars, planets, and moons that are millions and billions of miles away from us? Two words: Space exploration. The National Aeronautics and Space Administration (NASA) was created in 1958 to do just that. Their actual mission statement is "to pioneer the future in space exploration, scientific discovery and aeronautics research."

JUST IN CASE LIFE IS FOUND ON SOME OTHER PLANET, NASA HAS AN OFFICE OF PLANETARY PROTECTION. ONE OF ITS GOALS IS TO PROTECT ALIEN LIFE FROM EARTHLINGS.

Over the past 50 years, NASA has coordinated hundreds of space exploration projects. Those projects range from putting humans into space and on the moon, to sending remote vehicles to land on Mars and launching a spacecraft to Pluto. Every mission has the goal of gathering data and sending it back to Earth for scientists to learn more about our celestial neighborhood.

NASA isn't the only agency that launches exploration missions into space, but it does account for a lot of them. Space exploration is a global activity: The European Space Agency, Roscosmos (in Russia), and JAXA (in Japan) have been carrying out planetary exploration missions for decades. More recently, India and China have had successful missions, such as to the moon and Mars. South Korea, the United Arab Emirates, and Saudi Arabia are currently planning missions. Many of these countries cooperate with each other, offering a slot on their spacecraft to an instrument from another country.

An artist's depiction of NASA's MAVEN nearing Mars

The Atlas V rocket launches, carrying the Mars Science Lab and Curiosity.

3...2...1...BLASTOFF!

Long before a mission is ready to blast off into space, scientists and engineers design the vehicle. They must figure out the propulsion, power, telecommunications, avionics, and computer software engineering that each probe or spacecraft will need to carry out its mission.

Propulsion systems provide the energy to get the vehicle to its destination. For example, in order to deliver a Mars Exploration Rover (MER) to the red planet, a very large, heavy rocket was used to launch the rover into space. A power system gives energy to the rover itself as it maneuvers about the planet. On the MERs Spirit and Opportunity, this involves a solar-powered battery that is rechargeable, since replacing a regular battery on Mars isn't really an option.

The telecommunications system lets the spacecraft or probe communicate with the scientists back on Earth. This is a critical part of the mission. If the Mars rovers were unable to send back data, the entire mission would be worthless. Avionics refers to the computer "brain" of the spacecraft or rover. This is the electronics part that controls the overall movement of the rover, its deployment of different arms, and the memory where it saves all of the data it gathers. The last part is the software engineering. That's what allows the scientists on Earth to send commands to steer or guide the vehicle and collect data even though it is thousands or millions of miles away.

Once all of these systems are in place—something that can take years—the mission vehicle is ready to blast off!

ON THE WAY

So the spacecraft is hurtling through space toward its final destination. What happens when it gets there? When will it start gathering data? Will it land on a planet, moon, or

IT TOOK MORE THAN FIVE YEARS OF WORK AND 7,000 PEOPLE TO CREATE THE $2.5-BILLION MARS CURIOSITY ROVER.

comet? Or will it just orbit and take data from there? Well, that depends on the mission sequence. The mission sequence is a predetermined plan that details how and when the vehicle will conduct its tasks.

Not all missions can do everything. Here are some of the different ways that scientists can gather data from objects in space:

- **FLYBY:** to take pictures and gather data as a spacecraft speeds past an object
- **ORBIT:** to stay around the planet and take a full global map or study the weather from space
- **LAND:** to take measurements in one spot on the surface
- **ROVE:** to explore multiple locations on a surface and take measurements
- **RETURN SAMPLES:** to collect samples and then bring them back to Earth

The moon is the only celestial body where all of these have been done, but NASA is preparing a plan to bring samples back from Mars within the next decade.

Not every spacecraft sent out to explore the solar system can easily land on its object for study. The closest many probes can get to their designated planet or moon is a quick flyby or orbit. This was the case for NASA's New Horizons mission to Pluto, which zoomed past at 36,040 miles an hour (58,000 km/h)— more than 50 times faster than the speed of

sound on Earth—and used a radio system to send back to Earth the collected data. Another flyby is in the future: An upcoming Europa mission, currently slated to take place in the 2020s, will put a spacecraft in orbit around Jupiter. From there, the spacecraft will be able to collect valuable information about Jupiter's icy moon Europa, including information about the nature of its subsurface ocean and whether or not life could exist there.

EXPLORING FROM AFAR

So how do scientists gather data when they can't actually get test samples from the surface of the planet? Radar mapping is a great way to learn about the topography, or the physical features, of a planet from a distance. With radar imaging, scientists can see mountains, valleys, canyons, craters,

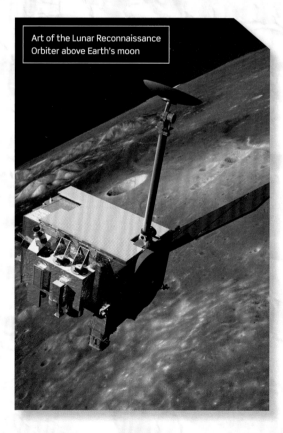

Art of the Lunar Reconnaissance Orbiter above Earth's moon

plains, and even lava flows. The radar produces an image of what the surface of the object looks like, even through a very thick atmosphere like on Venus or Titan. By looking at the topography, they can also create theories about past environments. A mountain with a rubbed-down top may experience erosion from high winds. And a dried-up bit of a valley may be the remnant of a lake that once held water.

Another way we can study planets from afar is to use infrared spectrometers. Infrared spectrometers use energy from a planet's surface—either as light reflected from the sun or as heat. Different minerals, ices, and gases reflect or emit energy differently. Each reflection or emission has a specific, or characteristic, pattern that can be used to identify what a planet is made of from afar. These give clues to what happened in the past, like the temperature of lava, the composition of gas, and even the temperature and chemistry of water.

SCIENTIST PROFILE

CARLE PIETERS

Dr. Carle Pieters is a professor at Brown University and was also the principal investigator of NASA's Moon Mineralogy Mapper, which was responsible for finding water on the moon. Dr. Pieters's research includes planetary exploration and the use of spectroscopy for compositional analysis. So what does that mean? It's her job to determine the chemical makeup of the moons, planets, or comets she explores.

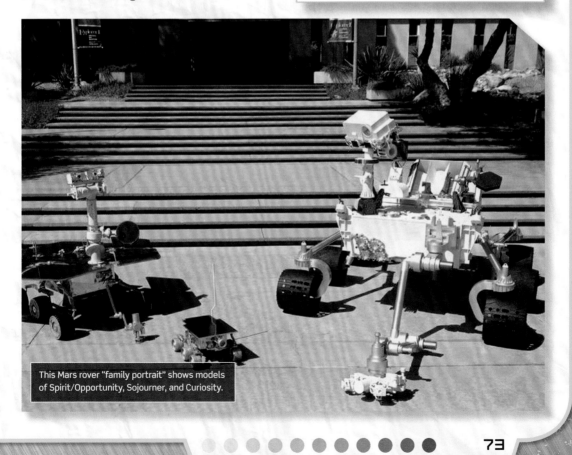

This Mars rover "family portrait" shows models of Spirit/Opportunity, Sojourner, and Curiosity.

BEEP! BEE

SHOOTING LASERS

Examining and testing different parts of soil on a planet millions of miles away is not easy—especially when you can't touch it with your hands. Scientists have developed a way for rovers, once landed on the surface, like Curiosity on Mars, to shoot a laser at rocks and soil to gather chemical data. It's called laser-induced breakdown spectroscopy, or LIBS. The laser puts so much energy into a small spot on the surface that it heats and forms a plasma—bits of ions, atoms, and small molecules that glow. The light from the glowing plasma is directed via telescope to the spectrometer. Then, the pattern caused by different chemical elements is analyzed to determine the types of minerals and trace elements in the soil or rock. Not a bad way to shed some light on the subject!

The Sample Analysis at Mars (SAM) instrument aboard Curiosity contains spectrometers to search for carbon and other elements.

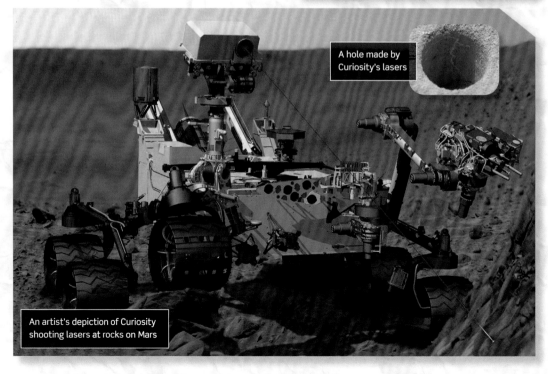

A hole made by Curiosity's lasers

An artist's depiction of Curiosity shooting lasers at rocks on Mars

Shadows cast by tall rock structures on Mars

CHECK THE SHADOW

Sometimes the only tool that scientists have to determine height or depth of an object is its shadow. If they measure the length of the shadow that is cast and compare it to the angle of the light source, it is possible to figure out an object's height or depth. This method works with both mountains and craters.

TRY THIS

COMPARE HEIGHTS WITH YOUR SHADOW

1. Find a place on the sidewalk or a driveway and have your friend trace your shadow in the exact same place three different times in a day. Trace your friend's shadow the same way. Good times to use would be 9:30 a.m., noon, and 3:30 p.m.

2. Note the height of each shadow in a notebook. How does the shadow's length change as the sun moves through the sky?

3. Now, compare it to your actual height and your friend's shadow. Can you tell by the shadows who is taller and by how much? How might this experiment compare to how scientists use shadows to measure objects on other planets?

MATERIALS:
- Chalk
- A sidewalk or driveway
- A friend or family member
- A ruler or measuring stick

MARS ROVER

LET'S TAKE A CLOSER LOOK INTO ONE MISSION IN PARTICULAR: MARS SCIENCE LAB.

THE MISSION

You probably know of the Mars Science Laboratory (MSL) mission because it sent the rover Curiosity to the red planet. Curiosity's job is to trek around Mars searching for evidence the planet can support or might have once supported life.

MSL is a roving mission, which means that Curiosity won't be returning to Earth with geologic samples from Mars. Instead, it sends data and images back to Earth via NASA's Deep Space Network—a network of antennas that span the globe.

STICKING THE LANDING

Landing Curiosity took some pretty careful planning. First, the spacecraft carrying the rover entered Mars's atmosphere, heading toward the surface at thousands of miles an hour. Then it needed to be slowed down so that it didn't crash on the surface. A massive parachute deployed first. The parachute was more than 100 feet (30 m) across and could withstand pressures of up to 65,000 pounds (29,480 kg). That's important, because there is very little atmosphere on Mars to help slow the descent using air resistance. Still, the parachute could only slow the rover's fall to about 200 miles an hour (322 km/h), far too fast for landing.

As the rover got closer to the surface, the spacecraft's outer shells, meant to protect the rover from Mars's atmosphere, fell away. This included the parachute, so the rover and the remaining spacecraft—called its "descent stage"—began to free-fall. As it fell, rockets fired to slow the whole system down, and the descent stage lowered the rover tucked inside onto Mars using strong cords. The remaining descent stage then rocketed hundreds of feet (m) away, to avoid falling on the newly deployed rover. This maneuver, called the Sky Crane, allowed Curiosity to touch down softly on its wheels and begin its mission.

THE SPACECRAFT ENTERS MARS'S ATMOSPHERE
AND FALLS TOWARD MARS'S SURFACE.

A MASSIVE PARACHUTE DEPLOYS
TO SLOW THE SPACECRAFT'S FALL.

THE HEAT SHIELD DETACHES.

THE PARACHUTE DETACHES AND
ROCKETS FIRE TO SLOW THE DESCENT.

THE REMAINING
DESCENT STAGE
SPACECRAFT
FLIES FAR AWAY TO
AVOID FALLING ON
CURIOSITY.

A STRONG CORD LOWERS CURIOSITY
ONTO MARS'S SURFACE.

HAVE LAB, WILL TRAVEL

The Mars rover Curiosity is one seriously high-tech robot. It's the size of a car and weighs 2,000 pounds (900 kg). All that machinery is packed with sensors, computers, and cameras that help the rover send images and data of its amazing discoveries.

The most widely used form of data collection from Curiosity is photo imaging—taking pictures. All exploration vehicles are equipped with multiple cameras. Curiosity has 17 cameras onboard. The rover takes pictures of the geology on Mars, and scientists study the pictures to identify different landforms. Then they compare the landforms to ones we might have here on Earth. The images can also be used to figure out the weather on Mars. For a planet known to have high winds, there will be clouds of dust and the mountaintops may look worn down. Swirling winds may be identified as a type of tornado-like activity, called a dust devil, and, of course, clues to the past presence of water are always something that scientists seek to find.

Curiosity also has 10 scientific instruments onboard, allowing it to do science experiments right there on the planet! Its weather station measures temperature, pressure, and wind. It's also built to take samples of the Mars surface and run them through two different laboratory instruments to measure the mineralogy, chemistry, water content, and carbon content of samples. Why do we care about carbon? Well, it's a building block of life as we know it. Other instruments will determine the amount of radiation on the planet, and figure out the chemical and mineral composition of rocks and soils at the surface without pulling them into the onboard lab. The rover is performing many of the tests scientists do in laboratories on Earth, without needing to bring people to the surface of Mars.

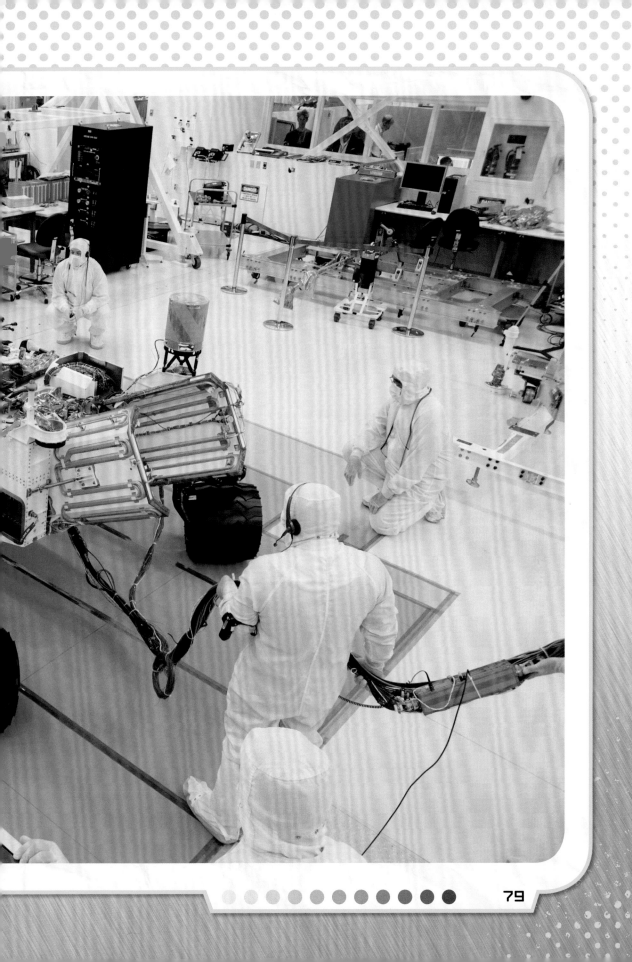

CRATERS

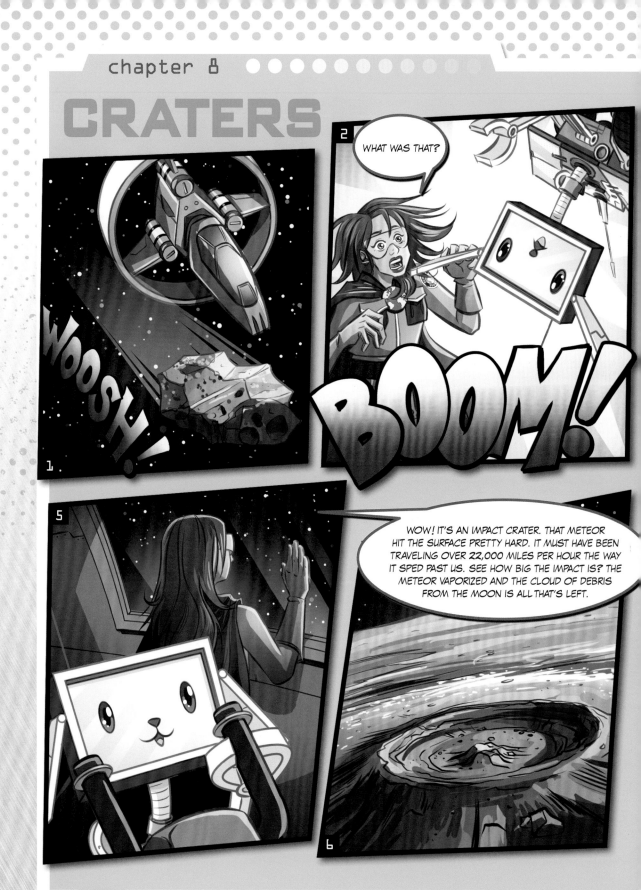

CRATERS

Ever go out when it's raining and make big puddles when you step into the mud? When that mud hardens and the water dries up, what have you left behind? A crater! Well, sort of. A crater is just an empty hole that is made by the impact of another object. So, you could say that your foot stomping in the wet mud created a kind of crater. Of course, that's not exactly how it works in space, but craters are the most common landform found in the solar system. Why? Because when everything was formed, a lot of rocks and bits of tiny planets broke apart and flew around, bumping into each other. As these pieces hit—or impacted— each other, craters were formed. That's why we call them impact craters.

Every planet in our solar system has craters. Many moons, asteroids, and even comets have them, too. By studying craters and counting how many there are on a surface, planetary geologists can figure out the age of an object's surface. Craters also churn up rocks from deep underground, revealing the composition of the planet beneath its outermost crust.

AMATEUR ASTRONOMERS FIRST TO SEE IMPACT

You don't have to be a trained scientist to study the stars. Grab your video camera and look to the skies! In 2010 not one, but two, amateur astronomers were the first people to see either a comet or asteroid run into Jupiter. The funny thing was that they were several thousands of miles apart. Christopher Go lives in the Philippines and Anthony Wesley lives in Australia. Both happened to be watching Jupiter when ... flash! ... they noticed a two-second splash of light. Christopher was lucky enough to get it on video. When they put the word out online, scientists studying Jupiter quickly looked through their data, too. They believe that the flash of light was a comet or asteroid burning up in the gaseous atmosphere of Jupiter. What a lucky sighting.

LOOK OUT!

When an asteroid hits a target, a massive amount of energy is released. Think of it this way: If a meteorite has a mass of 816 pounds (370 kg), and it is traveling through space at a speed of 22,816 miles an hour (36,720 km/h), the amount of kinetic energy due to its movement will be about 19 gigajoules (kinetic energy = 1/2 x mass x velocity). That is equal to the amount of energy used in the average American home in one month, or the same energy released when 4.8 tons (4.3 t) of TNT is exploded. In other words, when a crater is formed there will be a huge ... *boom!*

Immediately upon impact, the asteroid will create a hole and an enormous shock wave will pass through the target's surface. A jet of dust and particles is shot up from the impact. In the next few minutes, the shock wave will travel down beneath the surface and actually compress some of the crust. The asteroid and some of the target typically vaporize or melt because of the energy released during impact. The hole continues to grow to more than ten times the size of the asteroid depending upon how great the

TA-BAM!

THE LARGEST IMPACT BASIN ON THE MOON, KNOWN AS THE SOUTH POLE-AITKEN (SPA) BASIN, IS 1,550 MILES (2,500 KM) WIDE AND MORE THAN SEVEN MILES (12 KM) DEEP.

shock wave was. If the impact is deep, there is a large amount of debris thrown back—ejected—out of the hole, called "ejecta." This enlarges the crater even more. The rule is, the larger the asteroid and the faster it is traveling, the larger the crater. Some craters can be small, and span only a few feet. Others can be massive and measure more than 185 miles (300 km) across. Craters that large are called impact basins.

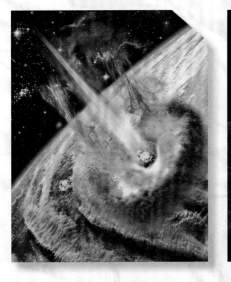

Artists imagine the energy released from asteroids' impacts on Earth.

AN ARTIST'S REPRESENTATION OF CHICXULUB CRATER, WHICH IS BURIED BENEATH THE YUCATÁN PENINSULA IN MEXICO. SCIENTISTS BELIEVE THE IMPACT BROUGHT ABOUT THE END OF THE AGE OF DINOSAURS.

MAKE YOUR OWN CRATER

You may want to do this outside or in a bathtub. It could get messy!

1. Put a 1- to 2-inch (2.54- to 5.08-cm) layer of flour into the pan.

2. Cover the flour with a thinner layer of the other powder. These are like the different layers of soil or rocks on the surface of the planet.

3. Hold one of your meteorites approximately 2 feet (0.6 m) over the pan.

4. Drop it. Record how deep the "crater" is.

5. Repeat with different round objects.

How does the weight of the object affect the size of the crater? How does the height the object is dropped from affect the size of the crater?

MATERIALS:
- A large shallow pan with edges
- Flour
- Dry pudding mix, powdered cocoa—or any dry powder that is different in color from the flour
- Several different round objects, such as nuts (almonds, peanuts), cherries, or marbles (These are your meteorites.)
- Ruler

POCKMARKED PLANET

Craters can be found on most planetary surfaces—some more than others. Mercury, part of Mars, and our own moon are covered with deep craters. Craters have even been found on some of the gas giants' icy moons. Despite the fact that its outer atmosphere is made mostly of gas, Jupiter showed damage from the comet Shoemaker-Levy 9, which hit the planet in 1994. When the comet hit the planet, it disrupted the layers of gas in its atmosphere, creating a dark spot. Earth, while it doesn't appear to have as many craters as the moon, still shows signs of impact. Scientists believe that Earth has been hit by more than 10 times the number of objects that have struck the moon. Scientists have run models that suggest that more than three million impact craters from 0.62 miles (1 km) in diameter to more than 620 miles (1,000 km) in diameter have existed on Earth.

Meteor crater, Flagstaff, Arizona, U.S.A.

Why can't we see them all anymore? The Earth's own geologic processes, such as erosion, volcanic eruptions, and plate subduction have erased most of the craters. One of the largest impact craters ever formed on Earth's surface is the Vredefort impact crater, which is found near Johannesburg, South Africa. This crater, which can still be seen today, was formed about two billion years ago. Its initial size is believed to have been 185 miles (300 km) across. That's 10 times as wide as the Grand Canyon.

COUNTING CRATERS

Since almost every planetary body has craters, many geologists are curious to learn more about them. Planetary geologists also count the number of craters on a planet, moon, or asteroid to tell how old it is. Many, many craters were formed by the impact of debris at the time the solar system began—about 4.5 billion years ago. Think about it—with all that debris flying around, many things would likely have hit each other. As the years went by, the big chunks were whittled into smaller chunks as pieces flew off. Some of the large pieces attracted other pieces, making them larger and turning them into planets, reducing the overall amount of debris. The pieces flying through space became fewer, so fewer impacts happened.

How does looking at an image of a bunch of craters on the surface of a planet help scientists determine its age? They figure that the portion of the surface of a planet with a lot of craters is probably much older than a portion of the planet with fewer craters. The older surface has more time to accumulate craters than the younger surface. A great example of this is Mars. The southern hemisphere of Mars has tons of craters—really big ones, too. That means it is an older portion of the planet. The northern area of Mars has fewer, and smaller, craters. Does that mean that part of the Mars surface is newer? Possibly. If you assume that all of Mars was created at once, then the whole planet

should be covered in craters, like the southern hemisphere. But it is not. Scientists believe that the northern hemisphere was filled in by volcanic lavas, filling in the craters originally there, making the surface a younger age than elsewhere on the planet.

Crater density, or the number of craters in a certain area, can be used to compare different celestial bodies. If you count the number of craters in a specific area on a particular planet like Mars, and then compare it to the number of craters on a similar-size object, say Earth's moon, then you can figure out the relative ages of the two bodies. Of course you also have to account for other factors, like distance from the asteroid belt or different impact velocities due to different gravities depending on the size of the body. To help set a baseline for calculating age, scientists use samples of moon rock, brought back by the Apollo astronauts, to calculate the moon's precise age.

EUGENE SHOEMAKER

Dr. Eugene Shoemaker created the study of astrogeology. He took Earth's principles of geology and applied them to the mapping of planets. You might say he was the first planetary geologist. His studies resulted in three decades of discoveries about the planets and asteroids of the solar system. Along with his wife, Carolyn, and science partner, David Levy, he discovered the comet Shoemaker-Levy, which impacted Jupiter in 1994, giving the world of science new insight into both the dynamics of comets and the planetary science of Jupiter.

THIS PHOTO SHOWS
SATURN'S MOON MIMAS
COVERED IN CRATERS.

YOU CAN COUNT CRATERS, TOO!

With the help of NASA and a computer program, you can count craters on the moon, Mars, and even Mercury. People can sign up to be planetary mappers. Who knows what they may discover through a computer or telescope?

THE MAJOR PARTS OF A CRATER

A CRATER IS MORE THAN JUST A BIG HOLE. IT IS MADE UP OF MANY DIFFERENT PARTS. LET'S STEP INSIDE ONE ON MARS AND CHECK IT OUT.

RIM: This is the edge at the top of the crater wall. It's usually in the shape of a circle or an ellipse, and it can sometimes curl over. The rim is made up of all the material that was pushed out of the way by the impact of the object that made the crater.

WALLS: These are ridges that surround the floor. They are usually pretty steep, too steep for someone to climb easily. The biggest, deepest crater on the moon has walls that stretch five miles (8 km) high!

RAYS: These are bits of rock and debris that were ejected from the land when the crater was formed. Sometimes they appear as streaks on the land surrounding the crater. Rays are not seen on every crater. Scientists think this is because they fade over time. So when you see a ray, it may be because the crater is rather young.

FLOOR: This is the bottom of the crater. It's usually bowl-shaped but can be flat, too. The floor can be bumpy and covered with rocks, or smooth like sand.

CENTRAL PEAK: Scientists aren't completely sure how the central peak forms. We've never seen an impact large enough to watch this happen. Most scientists think that the central peak is formed by a rebound effect. When an object hits the surface, the shock wave compresses the material. As the compressed material "bounces" back, the central peak is formed when the released material overshoots its position and then gravity pulls it back down into a pile. Think of a basketball being bounced into a frosted cake. The cake will have a dent, but some of the frosting may stick to the basketball as you pull it out. The frosting will most likely make a peak, like the central peak in a crater.

EJECTA: This is bits of earth, rocks, soil, or whatever was originally on the land where the crater hit. These pieces are thrown outside of the crater and eventually rest on the land around it, forming a blanket of material around the crater.

Satellite photo of Manicouagan crater

EARTHLY CRATERS

Most Earth craters are caused by an impact of a meteorite hitting the Earth. Some craters remain large, open holes, but others have mountains or ridges in the center. Still other craters fill up with rain and become lakes. Here are a few different types of craters that are found around the world.

Meteor crater is an impact crater that was created more than 50,000 years ago. It is more than three-quarters of a mile (about 1 km) wide and over 750 feet (229 m) deep. That is about the size of two football fields. It was caused when a 150-foot (46-m) meteorite made of nickel and iron hit the Earth.

The Spider crater is a complex crater found in western Australia. A complex crater is a crater with a central peak or ridge. The Spider crater is so named because it looks like a spider with all of its legs spread out in a fan shape. The spider legs are actually the remains of the central peak, which has been worn partway down by erosion. Spider crater is large, at over eight miles (13 km) wide, and was made between 600 and 900 million years ago.

The Lonar crater was created more than 50,000 years ago and is a simple impact crater. "Simple crater" means it does not have a central peak. Although that is difficult to tell now because there is so much rain in India, where the crater is located, that it filled

up with water. Now it is known as a lake. It stretches 1.1 miles (1.8 km) across and is approximately 500 feet (150 m) deep.

The Manicouagan crater in Quebec, Canada, is a complex crater. It was formed more than 212 million years ago. At 40 miles (65 km) across, it is one of the biggest craters on Earth. The asteroid that caused it hit the planet so hard that it melted large amounts of rock, which filled part of the crater. The huge shock waves also created multiple central rings instead of a peak. These look like concentric circles that expand out from the center. Over millions of years, erosion has worn down the crater, and a few of the central rings are now filled with water to create a ring lake.

This false-color photo of Spider crater shows the dry land in pink, including the crater's spiderlike legs.

CLIMATE AND THE IMPORTANCE OF WATER

CLIMATE
AND THE IMPORTANCE OF
WATER

Temperature, humidity, wind, rain, and cloudiness all tell you about the weather within your world. Weather, as we all know, is the play-by-play of events that happen in our atmosphere every day. Is it sunny? Is it cloudy or rainy? In contrast, climate gives you the average weather in a specific area over a period of

> ALMOST 97 PERCENT OF THE EARTH'S WATER IS SALTY, WHICH MEANS YOU CAN'T DRINK IT. SOME 2 PERCENT IS LOCKED UP IN GLACIERS AND ICE CAPS. THAT LEAVES ONLY 1 PERCENT OF ALL OF THE WATER ON THE PLANET THAT CAN BE USED FOR DRINKING.

time. While weather can change in an instant, climate typically changes very slowly. It can take hundreds or even thousands of years to change.

WATER RULES ALL

On Earth, one of the biggest contributors to our climate is water. More than 70 percent of the surface of our planet is covered with water. The water we have now is the same water that was here billions of years ago when Earth first formed. We may right now be feeling rain that once fell on the dinosaurs, or maybe on the pyramids of ancient Egypt. How is that possible? The water cycle. The water cycle is Earth's way of recycling the water on our planet.

The first step in the cycle is evaporation, when liquid water is turned into water vapor. Any liquid water can be vaporized, or turned into a gas. That includes water from plants, trees, rivers, lakes, streams, oceans, and snow. As the water vapor rises, it fills the atmosphere. The atmosphere can't

This lagoon sticks up above the water on the island of Fulaga, Fiji.

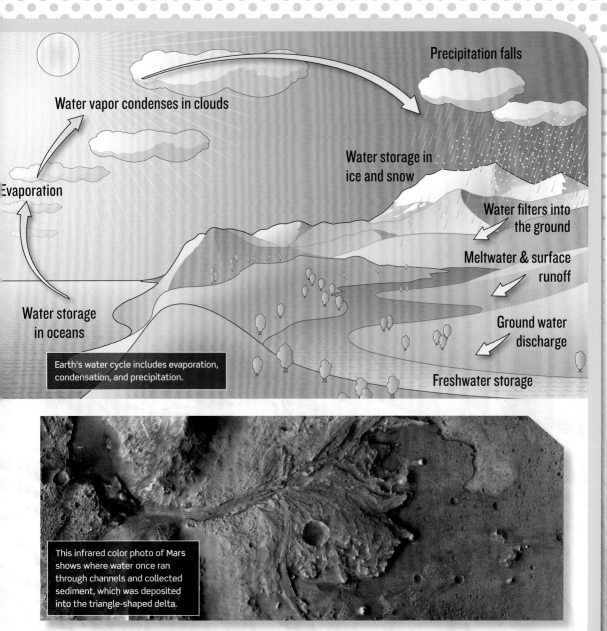

Water vapor condenses in clouds

Precipitation falls

Evaporation

Water storage in ice and snow

Water filters into the ground

Meltwater & surface runoff

Water storage in oceans

Ground water discharge

Freshwater storage

Earth's water cycle includes evaporation, condensation, and precipitation.

This infrared color photo of Mars shows where water once ran through channels and collected sediment, which was deposited into the triangle-shaped delta.

hold all of that water vapor, so it condenses, forming tiny droplets of water. These droplets appear as dew on the morning grass, or more often as clouds in the sky. As the clouds collect droplets of condensed water, the droplets become very heavy. Eventually they are too heavy and the clouds release the water as rain, sleet, or snow. This precipitation is the last step in the water cycle.

Temperature has a big effect on the water cycle. Warmer temperatures cause water on the surface to evaporate, which rises to form clouds. The result is precipitation in the form of rain. Colder temperatures can result in frozen precipitation like snow or sleet. As water falls to the ground, it can erode land, washing away dirt, or fill up streams, causing them to overflow. It can also enter the rocks and soil and collect under the Earth's surface, forming groundwater. Earth is a special planet because its abundance of water and resulting water cycle regulate our planet and allow it to sustain life.

This photo shows veins of salts that formed from groundwater flowing through rocks at the landing site of the Curiosity rover.

MINERAL FINGERPRINTS

Mars is one of the most studied planets. Scientists on Earth are naturally curious about the planet that is one of our closest neighbors. For many years, their focus has been to understand water on Mars. Enormous channels seen from space showed that water played a huge part in shaping the surface of Mars but until recently, they were not sure how long this lasted and whether the waters were fresh or salty. Then they began using a scientific technique called spectroscopy to study the planet. Spectroscopy is a scientific measurement of light. Every material absorbs, emits (gives off), or scatters light. Some do more than one of those. Each color of light has a certain wavelength, like those in a rainbow—remember ROYGBIV? When light is absorbed or reflected by materials, not all of the light acts in the same way. Only certain wavelengths of light get absorbed. Others get reflected. This is why an object looks red—because red is the color that is reflected back at us. The other colors are absorbed.

Scientists use spectroscopy to determine the types of minerals and gases that are present on a planet. If they know, for example, that a clay or salt mineral or carbon dioxide gas has a certain spectroscopy pattern—almost like a fingerprint—they can look for that when they scan the planet. These spectroscopic fingerprints of minerals and

HEY, THIS IS WHAT DR. EHLMANN DOES! SEE PAGE 112 TO LEARN MORE.

compounds tell them much about the composition of the surface.

In 2004, Mars researchers landed a rover on a spot identified by spectroscopy and found signs of past salty water that was in shallow lakes and underground. The Opportunity rover found sedimentary rocks with iron oxide and sulfate salts in them. The rocks had ripples from an ancient lake shoreline. Mineral fingerprints had led the team to water!

SUSPICIOUS STREAKS

More than 10 years later, scientists were studying new data from high-resolution images and noticed something strange. Dark streaks on certain mountain slopes on Mars appear to get darker and lighter over time. Could this possibly be water ebbing and flowing as the temperatures change? The streaks seemed to become active at temperatures right around the melting point of water ice. If so, that would be similar to what happens here on Earth when snow melts and flows down mountainsides. Upon closer inspection, it looked like the streaks could be small streams of water containing a lot of salts and minerals. This discovery is exciting to say the least, and one that has renewed the efforts of researchers in their quest to find liquid water on the red planet.

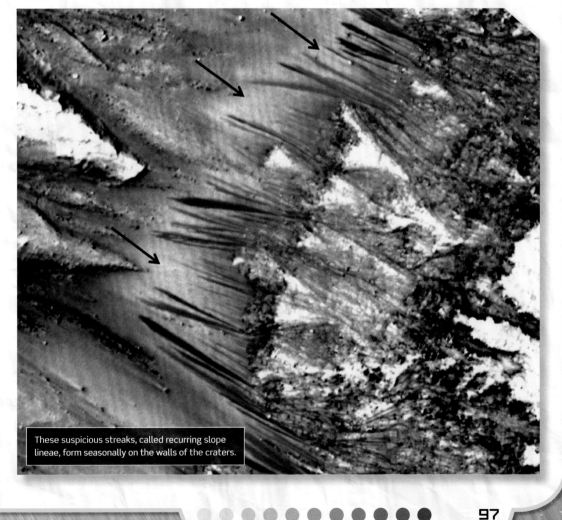

These suspicious streaks, called recurring slope lineae, form seasonally on the walls of the craters.

TITAN'S LAKES

Saturn's moon Titan is the only celestial body in our solar system besides Earth to have lakes and seas on its surface. The big difference? Titan's seas and lakes are filled with methane and ethane, both hydrocarbons that might be good for some organisms but would be toxic for humans. Since

THE METHANE-ETHANE MIXTURE IN TITAN'S LAKE IS MADE OF HYDROCARBONS SIMILAR TO THE GAS THAT YOU USE IN YOUR CAR.

Titan's surface temperatures reach a frosty minus 292°F (-180°C), it's not surprising there is no liquid water there. Water at that temperature is frozen. Liquid methane and ethane, which have freezing points much lower than the temperatures on Titan's surface, remain in liquid form in the lakes and seas.

One question scientists are exploring is whether Titan has a methane-ethane cycle similar to that of the water cycle on Earth. The answer is—they think so. With its clouds, seas, and oceans, it is fairly safe to assume that it has rain, too. In fact, scientists believe that Titan may even have aquifers—underground concentrations of methane and ethane, which may fill up indentations that occur on the surface. The same process takes place here on Earth with natural springs.

HOW DEEP IS YOUR LAKE?

Finding the depth of a lake on Earth is easy. You simply use sonar, which is underwater radar, to bounce sound off of the bottom of the lake to get a good picture. Then you calculate volume by multiplying length, width, and height.

Finding the depth of a lake on a moon millions of miles away isn't so easy. Scientists use radar to calculate the size of the lake, but they can only penetrate so far. The radar signal travels forward until it is reflected back up—but did it reflect off the bottom of the lake? Since the lake is on a distant celestial body, no one knows. Instead, they must use clues from the topography of the land surrounding the lake. Is the lake at the top of a mountain? Is the land sloped at a steep angle or a shallow angle? All of this information is compiled and a best guess is made about the depth.

An artist's rendition of ice forming on a hydrocarbon sea on Titan

RAIN ON OTHER PLANETS

While Earth may be the only planet to have vast amounts of liquid water on its surface, it is not the only one that experiences rain. Scientists believe that Jupiter might have helium rain. Helium, the kind of gas that we put into balloons to make them float, is abundant in the atmosphere on the large planet. So is neon, another gas we are familiar with (it was once used to advertise businesses with brightly lit neon lights).

Both neon and helium are found in the central atmosphere of Jupiter, but neon is curiously absent from the upper atmosphere. The reason? Perhaps the neon mixes with helium and falls like rain onto the planet's surface.

IT'S PROBABLY A GOOD THING THAT IT DOESN'T RAIN ON VENUS. ITS CLOUDS ARE MADE OF SULFURIC ACID.

IS IT RAINING DIAMONDS?

Research has shown that if you were to visit Saturn you may come back richer than you ever imagined. It is possible that chunks of diamonds may be floating around in the planet's atmosphere. Diamonds are formed when the element carbon, commonly found as soot or graphite (which is similar to the graphite in your pencil), is subjected to extreme heat and pressure. Lightning storms on Saturn turn methane that contains carbon into soot, and eventually graphite. The graphite is heated to the point where it could form diamonds that fall from the sky. Thus—diamond rain. Is it true? No one can know for sure until a sample is captured. But when a spacecraft does visit to gather samples, scientists on Earth should be ready to bring home a very precious and expensive prize.

TRY THIS

MAKE A MINI WATER CYCLE

MATERIALS:
- A mug
- A plastic mixing bowl taller than the mug
- Water
- Plastic cling wrap
- Large rubber band

1. Place the mug in the bowl.

2. Add water around the mug until it comes about two-thirds of the way up the mug.

3. Cover the bowl with cling wrap and fasten it tightly to the bowl by wrapping the rubber band around the plastic.

4. Place the bowl in a sunny area and watch what happens.

Over a few hours, you should see water begin to condense on the cling wrap. Eventually, you will see water in the mug. This came from precipitation.

AVALANCHE!

When we hear the word "avalanche," we think of big chunks of snow cascading down a huge mountaintop. That process happens here on Earth, but what about on Mars? Does it have avalanches? Wait, Mars doesn't even have snow, does it? Yes, it does. Well, sort of. Snow of the wet, fluffy, frozen-ice kind we see on Earth does not currently fall on Mars. What Mars does have at its poles is snow made of frozen carbon dioxide. To us, that would be like flakes of dry ice, the substance that entertainers use on stage to create mysterious clouds or fog. Mars also has thick slabs of water ice that make up the bulk of its polar caps. Where there are piles of snow and ice, there are avalanches. In 2015, an avalanche stretching 65 feet (20 m) across was seen happening on the edge of Mars's north pole. Avalanches are definitely tools of erosion, as they take bits of rock and soil with them while they fall. By studying the rate of erosion on Mars, scientists hope to learn more about how those same systems—which include water, carbon dioxide, ices, and gases—may work on our own planet. It may also tell us about the stability of the ice caps on Mars. Is Mars coming out of an ice age and losing mass from its caps? With more measurements, we will soon find out.

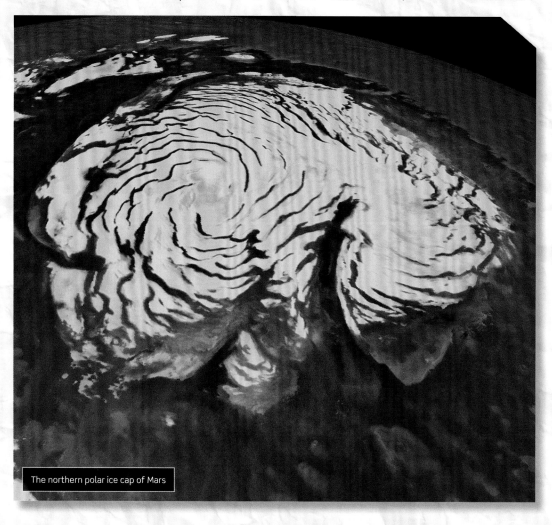

The northern polar ice cap of Mars

These photos show the effects (before, top; during, center; and after, bottom) of seasonal avalanches on dunes on Mars.

ONLY THE BEGINNING

Earth is such a great place for us because it has everything needed to sustain life. It has a stable atmosphere and a magnetic field that protect us from the sun's radiation and strong solar winds, and yet it allows in heat and light for warmth and for plants to grow. The water cycle maintains a constant amount of water within our planet by way of a continuous recycling system: evaporation, condensation, and precipitation. Weathering and erosion processes repurpose rocks and organic matter, transporting them from the tops of mountains to the bottom of the ocean. This keeps our environment dynamic and ever changing. Earth also is located in what scientists call the habitable zone of our solar system. It contains the perfect environment for life. We seek to find this same mix of conditions elsewhere. In searching, it is a way to answer the questions we have—"are we alone?" and "what is our future?"—when we look up into the sky.

Our home planet has everything we need to survive.

STUDYING SPACE ON EARTH

When you can't conduct research on the planet or moon you are studying, sometimes finding a hidden lake on Earth is the next best thing. Take a team of Russian scientists. After spending more than 10 years drilling, they have finally hit ice water. Surprising? Not to them. It's exactly what they expected to find. After all, they were drilling through Antarctic ice. The body of water they tapped, called Lake Vostok, is thought to have been buried beneath the ice for more than 14 million years.

Scientists think Lake Vostok's icy depths mirror the conditions of the ocean on Europa. Not only does Lake Vostok appear to be as deep as 10 miles (16 km), it also has traces of iron and sulfur, both elements believed to be in Europa's ocean. By conducting experiments in Lake Vostok, scientists are hoping they can discover more secrets about the ocean on the moon of Jupiter millions of miles away in space.

SCIENTIST PROFILE

SANJEEV GUPTA

As a professor of earth science at Imperial College in London, England, Dr. Sanjeev Gupta studies the history of landforms. He wants to reconstruct past landscapes and to figure out how—and why—they changed into the landscapes we know today. It was his work with the seafloor of the English Channel that led him to Mars. Surprisingly, the floor of the English Channel looks a lot like big channels on the surface of Mars. Soon NASA tapped him to help select landing sites for the Mars rovers. Today, he helps plan Curiosity's path as it explores Mars.

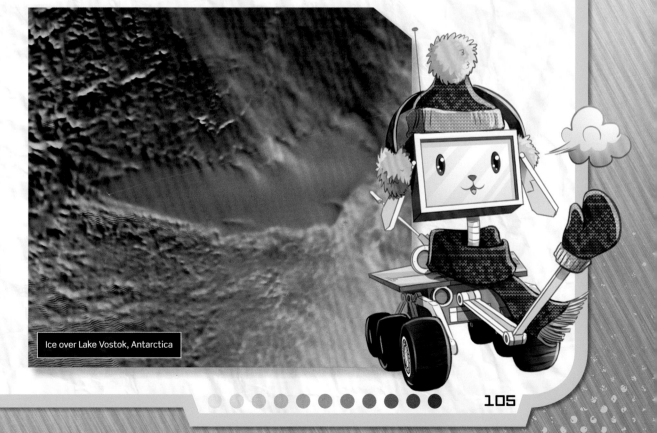

Ice over Lake Vostok, Antarctica

NASA'S "FAR OUT" PLANS
FOR FUTURE SPACE RESEARCH

NASA knows that the potential for research in space is unlimited. There are vast worlds to explore within our own solar system and beyond. But with so many possibilities, and only so much money, it's tough to figure out where to focus your attention. Will any of their projects work? As the saying goes, you never know until you try.

Take a look at a few of the "far out" ideas that NASA is considering for future space research.

1 Submarine for Titan—This plan calls for a submarine to probe the depths of the icy lake on Titan. The catch? The submarine must be able to withstand the super cold methane-ethane mix in Kraken Mare, the 720-mile (1,159-km)-long lake. Not to mention the almost 900-million-mile (1.4-billion-km) trip and the frigid surface temperature: minus 290°F (-179°C).

2 Comet hitchhiker—A spacecraft that would harpoon itself to a passing comet and latch on for a ride as the comet streaks by in its orbit around the sun. The whole time it is sending back data to scientists on Earth about the comet and any celestial bodies it may fly by.

3 Humans on Mars—NASA hopes to send astronauts to Mars within the next few decades. On Mars, humans could investigate in person to answer some of our biggest questions: Is there liquid water? Is there or has there ever been life?

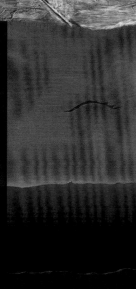

4 Europa Deep Drill—Scientists and engineers have been trying to figure out how to get through Europa's thick icy shell to the ocean underneath. One idea would be to send a "penetrator probe" that would intentionally crash into Europa, burying itself in the ice. Then a heated drill would extend from the probe and melt-drill its way through to the ocean.

5 Venus balloon— Since Venus's surface is hot enough to melt lead, it would be hard to send a rover. So why not send balloons? The balloons' shiny surfaces would reflect sunlight, helping to keep them cool, while they hover in Venus's atmosphere measuring its winds and chemicals.

LIFE DIFFERENT FROM OURS

Will our search for life as we understand it end in success? No one knows. But some scientists are thinking that we need to open our minds to the possibility that life might exist in a different form from ours. Perhaps life exists without water, as in the case of Titan's sea of methane and ethane.

What if the building blocks of life—cells—could be based not upon water, but organic compounds with nitrogen? You are already exposed to nitrogen on a daily basis. It makes up 80 percent of Earth's atmosphere. Nitrogen on Earth is recycled from the atmosphere, through plants that live and then die. Nitrogen enters the soil and eventually is taken up by a plant and released into the atmosphere. Nitrogen is as necessary as water for life on Earth. If you think of it that way, is it such a stretch to believe that cells can be formed based on nitrogen instead of water and carbon? Scientists at Cornell University are using computer models to show that it might be possible. At the moment these are only theories, but who knows? Perhaps someday spacecraft will be trolling the Titan surface for nitrogen-based beings.

Will we ever find life on another planet? Maybe! In our solar system, we're just beginning to explore Mars and the icy moons. Life as sophisticated as humans likely won't be found, but small microbes may be out there. We also are using telescopes to peer at other planets far outside our solar system, looking for other planets around other stars that might host life. If we keep searching, studying, and exploring, perhaps we will find one day that we do have neighbors, even very faraway ones, in our universe.

Traveling to Mars might reveal that life existed there.

Opening up our definition of life—and what
life needs to survive—can help us look for
life in the solar system and beyond.

LIKELY PLACES FOR ALIEN LIFE

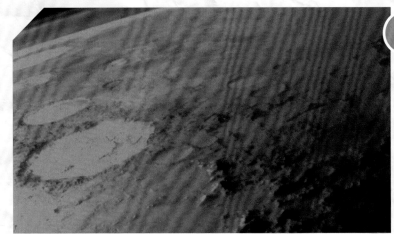

1 MARS

Its seasonal dark stripes might indicate salty water leaking out of its dust-covered surface.

2 ENCELADUS

With its spewing ice geysers, it is possible that a vast ocean of liquid water lies below the icy, cracked surface of Saturn's sixth largest moon.

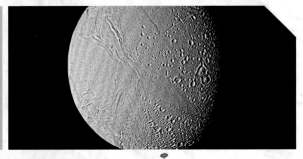

3 TITAN

Saturn's largest moon is the only place in our solar system, besides Earth, with liquid lakes. The fact that there is liquid may lead to life, although it is not an environment where humans could exist.

4 EUROPA

《《《

One of Jupiter's moons, it is said to have an icy ocean underneath 10 miles (16 km) of ice. It is possible organisms have found a way to exist within the cold darkness of its depths.

5 VENUS

》》》

Earth's sister planet has surface temperatures that are scorching hot, but its atmospheric temperatures are around 167°F (75°C). Could life exist floating around in the atmosphere? Perhaps.

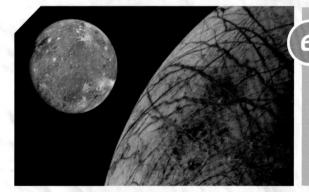

6 CALLISTO AND GANYMEDE

《《《

The twin moons of Jupiter may also have deeply buried oceans of liquid water beneath their 60 miles (97 km) of rock. Where there is water, there could be life.

7 TRAPPIST-1

》》》

With seven Earthlike planets and three within their sun's habitable zone, these rocky worlds could be home to life, or at least be home to conditions that could support life.

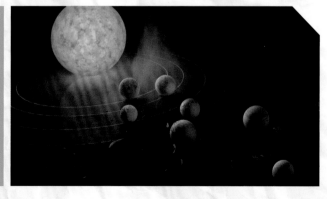

ALL ABOUT SPECTRA

How can you tell what rocks and soils are made of on other planets? It's really hard to tell if you can't go up close and look yourself. So, scientists developed a way to use light to tell what chemicals make up rocks and soils. It's called spectroscopy.

Spectroscopy is the study of how light is reflected or emitted at different wavelengths by materials. Some light we can see with our eyes. We call that "visible light." Visible light is made up of wavelengths that appear to us as the colors of the rainbow—red, orange, yellow, green, blue, and violet. Other wavelengths of light we can't see. Those include radio waves, microwaves, and infrared waves, among others. We can't see them, but we can measure them with instruments!

In spectroscopy of light, we're looking for specific patterns of light by wavelength. Every kind of chemical or mineral displays a characteristic spectrum. A spectrum (or "spectra" for more than one) is the pattern of highs and lows in light that are caused by a particular molecule. Spectra are like fingerprints for chemicals and minerals. Because these fingerprints are in light, we can use them to tell—even from far away—what chemicals and minerals are making up the materials we're looking at.

Spectroscopy can be used to study all kinds of different materials. Some people use spectra to study atmospheres. I use it to study rocks and soils. My work is all about tracing the history of planets in the solar system using the fingerprints of what they are made of, which are revealed by different types of spectroscopy. Here are three real examples.

1 THE FINGERPRINTS OF UNDERGROUND WATER ON MARS

From Mars's orbit, the Compact Reconnaissance Imaging Spectrometer for Mars (CRISM) on the Mars Reconnaissance Orbiter takes pictures of the Mars surface. Except, it doesn't just do this in wavelengths your eye can see. CRISM takes a picture in hundreds of wavelengths at the same time. That means for each pixel (or tiny bit of the photo), CRISM captures the whole spectrum of light of the materials it's photographing. We can use these fingerprints in the spectrum to identify the minerals.

For example, here's a spot on Mars called Nili Fossae, as shown in visible light. It's an image that shows an area about 3.7 miles (6 km) wide and is taken from 180 miles (289.7 km) away. This is what it would

look like if you were floating above the surface of Mars, looking down at it. You see a lot of red Mars dust, but you can't tell what the rocks underneath really look like.

But here's the same spot using infrared light. See all the colors that are there? That's CRISM capturing the mineral spectra of the rocks.

When I look at that infrared image, I don't just see pretty colors. I take a good look at what the colors are telling me. Each color is a different type of mineral, and how much of the color that's there tells me how much of the mineral is there. Using all the hundreds of wavelengths of light that this photo was taken

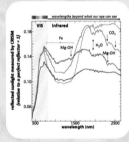

in, I can make a chart like this for those hundreds of wavelengths for each of the green, blue, yellow, and purple areas.

The photos and the chart tell me a lot. The specific fingerprints of reflected light that I see in this chart (along with all I learned about fingerprints from studying rocks on Earth!) tell me that the green areas are magnesium carbonate-rich rocks. The grayish blue areas are iron and magnesium clay rocks. The yellow color shows a mineral called olivine in volcanic rocks. The purple are volcanic rocks without olivine.

The rocks originally formed from lavas. The clays, which are minerals that contain water molecules, are in ridges that formed when water flowed underground. The water filled fractures in these rocks with the minerals we see now. The carbonates formed when water near the surface of Mars came into contact with Mars's carbon dioxide-rich atmosphere.

2 THE FINGERPRINTS OF PAST LAKE WATERS ON MARS

We use a different kind of spectrometer, called ChemCam, on the Mars rover Curiosity. ChemCam is a laser-induced breakdown spectrometer. Instead of using gentle sunlight, we actively shoot rocks and soils with a laser! The energy and heat create a plasma and excite the atoms of different chemicals in the rock into ions. As these ions go back into less excited states after we stop firing the laser, each kind emits light at specific wavelengths of light. These spectra of the light emissions are the fingerprints for the chemicals present in the rocks.

For example, we used ChemCam to look at a lake bed on Mars. Here's the three-foot (0.9-m)-wide area, as seen in visible light.

Using ChemCam data taken from shooting a laser at the small white veins in the rock, we were able to create this graph.

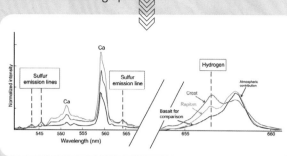

The spectrum of light tells us that there are hydrated calcium sulfate salts in the Mars rocks here. They formed as waters in the ancient lake evaporated into the atmosphere, leaving behind the salts.

3 WATER AND SALTS UNDERGROUND ON CERES

Spectroscopy is not just used on Mars. One of the most fun and exciting discoveries I was a part of recently was made on Ceres, a dwarf planet in the asteroid belt. Working with my colleagues on the Dawn mission, which includes the Visual and InfraRed (VIR) Mapping Spectrometer, we wanted to know what Ceres' mysterious bright spots are made of. Using spectra from VIR, taken in orbit, and carefully comparing them to data from Earth laboratories, we discovered the bright spots are usually a mix of sodium carbonate salts and ammonium salts. One even has some water ice. This was exciting because the spots formed recently, indicating relatively modern water on very cold Ceres. The heat to melt some of the salty ice beneath the crater was probably caused by impact from a giant asteroid.

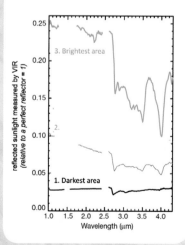

GLOSSARY

Aeronautics (air-o-NOT-iks): the science or engineering of flight

Aerospace: the science or engineering of spaceflight

Air resistance: the opposition offered by air to objects moving through it

Ammonia: a gas at Earth temperatures and ice at Pluto temperatures that is part nitrogen and part hydrogen

Analyses (un-AL-uh-sees): the examination of the parts or elements of an object

Antenna: a device, such as a rod or wire, for sending or receiving radio waves

Asteroid: a small, rocky celestial body orbiting the sun

Asteroid belt: the ring of space between the orbits of Mars and Jupiter where there are many asteroids

Astronomer: a person who studies the science of the celestial bodies and their sizes, motions, and composition

Atmosphere: a mass of gases surrounding a celestial body such as a planet

Atmospheric pressure: the pressure exerted by the weight of any given atmosphere

Avionics (A-vee-ON-iks): the computer "brain" of a spacecraft

Basalt rock: a type of rock that is dark gray in color, fine-grained, rich in iron and magnesium, and formed by the hardening of melted rock

Carbon: a common element on Earth, and one of the building blocks of life

Carbon dioxide: a gas at Earth temperatures and ice at Pluto temperatures that is part carbon and part oxygen. It is given off by

Ceres

humans and other animals and absorbed by plants.

Celestial body (suh-LESS-t-al): a natural object that is visible in the sky or universe

Ceres (SEER-eez): the only dwarf planet found in the asteroid belt between Mars and Jupiter

Charon (SHARE-on): a moon in synchronous orbit with the dwarf planet Pluto

Climate: the average weather conditions of a particular place or region over a period of years

Coma: a cloud of gas that forms when ice on a comet heats up

Comet: a celestial body made of a nucleus of ice and dust that has a tail of gas and dust particles when passing near the sun

Composition: the chemical makeup of an object or celestial body

Compositional analysis: the process of figuring out what chemicals planets, moons, or comets are made of

Constellation: a recognized group of stars forming a pattern

Convection current: the motion in a fluid in which the warmer portions rise and the colder portions sink

Convergent boundary: the location where two tectonic plates smash into one another (and either create mountains or one plate slides under the other)

Cosmic: the condition of or relating to our vast universe

Crater: a hole made by a large impact, such as a meteorite hitting a moon or planet

Crevice: a crack in a rock layer

Crust: the rocky outer layer of a planet

Cryovolcano: a volcano that erupts ice and water rather than lava

Debris: the remains of something, such as a rock, that is broken down or destroyed

Descent: the act or process of moving downward

Chicxulub crater

Divergent boundary: an area between two tectonic plates that are moving apart where magma comes up to fill the empty space and create new rock

Dwarf planet: a large object in our solar system without enough gravity to clear its orbit of other clumps of ice and dirt

Dwarf star: a star of relatively small size and low luminosity.

Earth: the planet on which we live

Electromagnetic waves: the natural radiation of waves of light, such as radio, infrared, visible light, ultraviolet, and x-ray, that are formed when an object releases energy

Ellipse (ih-LIPS): an oval orbit or shape

Enceladus (in-SELL-i-dus): the sixth largest moon of Saturn

Eris (AIR-is): the most massive and second largest dwarf planet in the solar system

Erosion (e-ROW-shun): the weathering of landforms caused mostly by wind or water

Europa (Ur-O-pa): the fourth largest moon of Jupiter

Evaporation: to turn liquid into a vapor or gas

Exoplanet: a planet in a solar system other than our own

Flyby: a flight of a spacecraft past a celestial body that is close enough to obtain scientific information

Fracture: a separation in a geologic formation that divides the rock into two or more pieces, sometimes forming a deep fissure or crevice

Galaxy: a large group of stars and other matter that is found somewhere in the universe

Gas: a state of matter that has no fixed shape and tends to expand to fill space

Gas giants: the four outer planets of our solar system, which are large and made up mostly of gases such as hydrogen and helium

Geologist: a person who studies rocks to learn about the history of Earth or another celestial body

Geology: the study of the features of a celestial body or the history of the Earth and its life as recorded in rocks

Gravity: a force of attraction between particles or bodies that occurs because of their mass

Habitable: suitable or fit to live in or on

Haumea (HOW-me-ya): a dwarf planet and the third-brightest object in the Kuiper belt

Heliocentric (heel-i-o-CENT-rik): the theory that the sun is the center of our solar system

Helium: a light, colorless, nonflammable element that is a gas

Humidity: the amount of moisture in the air

Hydrogen: a colorless, odorless, flammable gas

Igneous rock: the type of rock that comes from a volcano

Impact basin: a crater that is more than 185 miles (300 km) across

Infrared spectroscopy (spek-TRAW-ska-pee): a type of analysis that determines the chemistry of materials by measuring electromagnetic waves in the infrared range

Interplanetary: the space between planets

Jupiter: the largest of the planets in our solar system and fifth from the sun

Kinetic (kih-NET-ik) energy: the type of energy associated with motion

Kuiper (KY-per) belt: an area of the solar system beyond Neptune with dwarf planets and pieces of ice and rock

Landform: a natural feature of a land surface

Light-year: the distance light travels in one year, about 5.9 trillion miles (9.5 trillion km)

Magma: the molten rock material within the Earth

Magnetic field: the space near a magnetic body or a body carrying an electric current within which the magnetic forces can be detected

Magnetometer: an instrument used to measure the strength of a magnetic field

Makemake: a dwarf planet in the Kuiper belt

Jupiter

Mantle: the portion of a planet lying between the crust and the core

Mars: the fourth planet from the sun

Mars rover Curiosity: a car-size vehicle with scientific instruments sent to study Mars

Mercury: the smallest planet, and the one closest to the sun

Meteor: a very small celestial body that burns up in Earth's atmosphere, causing it to glow brightly for a short time

Meteor shower: a large group of meteors burning up in Earth's atmosphere from the same point in the night sky

Meteorite: a meteor that has landed on Earth's surface

Meteoroid: a rocky celestial body that is significantly smaller than an asteroid

Methane: a gas at Earth temperatures and ice at Pluto temperatures that is part carbon and part hydrogen

Milky Way: our galaxy

Minerals: the group of naturally occurring elements or compounds that form crystals

Mission: a specific aerospace task

Moon: a celestial body that orbits larger celestial bodies

NASA: the National Aeronautics and Space Administration

Nebulae (NEH-bu-lee): clouds of gases and dust that form the beginnings of solar systems

Neptune: the eighth planet from the sun

Nitrogen: a chemical element that also forms a gas or an ice and makes up 78 percent of Earth's atmosphere

Nuclear fusion reaction: to fuse together two atomic nuclei to create a larger nucleus and in the process release energy, like our sun does

Oort cloud: a collection of many icy objects in orbit around the sun

Orbit: the curved path of a celestial object or spacecraft around a star, planet, or moon

Mars rover Curiosity

Parachute: a device used to slow the motion of an object through an atmosphere by creating drag

Photosphere: the outer portion of the sun from which light and heat radiate

Planet: a celestial body that orbits the sun or another star but isn't a comet, asteroid, or satellite, such as a moon

Planet Nine: a possible giant ninth planet in the outer region of our solar system

Planetesimals (pla-nuh-TEH-seh-muhls): the beginnings of tiny new planets

Plasma: a state of matter formed from a collection of charged particles that is like a gas but conducts electricity and is affected by magnetic fields

Plutoid: a dwarf planet found in orbits farther from the sun than Pluto

Precipitation: material that falls to the surface of a planet as hail, mist, rain, sleet, or snow

Probe: a device used to penetrate or send back information, especially from outer space

Propulsion: the act of pushing an object forward in space

Radiation: the process of giving off radiant energy in the form of waves or particles

Rover: a space exploration vehicle designed to move across the surface of a planet or other celestial body

Satellite: a celestial body orbiting another of larger size

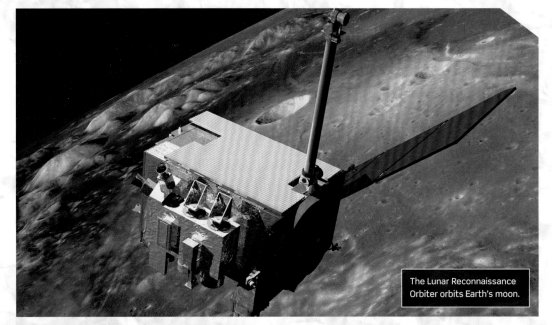

The Lunar Reconnaissance Orbiter orbits Earth's moon.

Plate tectonics: the theory that a few large crustal plates on a planet's or moon's outer surface move over time

Plumes: the risings of hot rock, ice, water, or other material through cracks in a planet's or moon's crust

Pluto: a dwarf planet in the Kuiper belt beyond Neptune

Saturn: the sixth planet from the sun

Shock wave: a wave formed by the sudden compression (as during a meteorite impact) of the substance through which the wave travels

Solar system: a star with the group of celestial bodies that revolve around it; in our case, the sun with its planets, moons, asteroids, and comets

Space suit: a suit made to make life in space possible for its wearer

Spacecraft: a vehicle for travel beyond the Earth's atmosphere

Spectroscopy (spek-TRAW-ska-pee): a measurement of light seen through or bounced back from surfaces or gases

Subduction: one tectonic plate being shoved beneath another

Sulfuric (sol-FUR-ik) acid: a strong acid that is colorless when pure and eats away at many solid substances

Supernova: the explosion of a star

Synchronous (SIN-kron-us) orbit: an orbit of two objects moving together as they circle a third object

Telecommunications: a way of communicating over distance by cable, telegraph, telephone, or broadcasting

Telescope: an instrument that helps scientists see into and beyond our solar system

Terrain: the surface features of an area of land

Thermal: designed to save or keep in heat

Thermometer: an instrument for measuring temperature

Tholins: carbon-containing molecules created from gases by solar ultraviolet radiation

Topography (tuh-PAH-gruh-fee): the heights of the physical features of a planet

Universe: the entire collection of things observed and unknown in space

Uranus: the seventh planet from the sun

Vaporize: to turn solid or liquid into a gas

Venus: the second planet from the sun

Volcanic vent: an opening in the crust from which lava, ash, and hot gases escape during an eruption

Remnants of a supernova, as captured by the Hubble Space Telescope

RESOURCES

Books

Aguilar, David A. *Alien Worlds: Your Guide to Extraterrestrial Life.* National Geographic Kids, 2013.

Aguilar, David A. *13 Planets: The Latest View of the Solar System.* National Geographic Kids, 2011.

Aguilar, David A., Christine Pulliam, and Patricia Daniels. *Space Encyclopedia: A Tour of Our Solar System and Beyond.* National Geographic Kids, 2013.

Aldrin, Buzz, and Marianne J. Dyson. *Welcome to Mars: Making a Home on the Red Planet.* National Geographic Kids, 2015.

Becker, Helaine, and Brendan Mullan. *Everything Space.* National Geographic Kids, 2015.

Carney, Elizabeth. *Mars: The Red Planet.* National Geographic Kids, 2016.

Schneider, Howard. *Ultimate Explorer Field Guide: Night Sky: Find Adventure! Go Outside! Have Fun! Be a Backyard Stargazer!* National Geographic Kids, 2016.

Websites

Astronomy for Kids
kidsastronomy.com/stars.htm

European Space Agency (ESA) for Kids
esa.int/esaKIDSen

NASA Kids' Club
nasa.gov/kidsclub/index.html

Planets for Kids
planetsforkids.org/

Solar System
interactivesites.weebly.com/solar-system.html

Space for Kids
kids.usa.gov/science/space/index.shtml

● Science **SUPERHEROES** ●

CHECK OUT ANOTHER SCIENCE SUPERHERO!

Tomecek, Steve. *Dirtmeister's Nitty Gritty Planet Earth.* National Geographic Kids, 2015.

BELOW SATURN'S RINGS, ITS
MOON MIMAS APPEARS AS A
TINY DOT.

INDEX

Boldface indicates illustrations.

A

Alexander, Claudia 29, **29**
Apollo mission 86
Asteroid belt **16,** 17, 22, 24, 114
Asteroids 26, **26,** 82, **82,** 83, **83,** 114
Atlas V rocket **71**
Avalanches, on Mars 100, **101**
Avionics 71, 114

B

Batygin, Konstantin 13, **13**
Big Dipper (star pattern) **31**
Brahe, Tycho 15
Brown, Mike 13, **13**
Burr, Devon 56, 58, **58**

C

Callisto (Jupiter's moon) 65, 111, **111**
Caloris Basin, Mercury 35, **35**
Cassini-Huygens Spacecraft 58
Cassini spacecraft 40, **40,** 46, **57, 121**
Ceres (dwarf planet) **27, 114**
    in asteroid belt 17, 22, 24
    classification 13
    defined 115
    name 27
    overview 24, **24**
    in solar system **16**
    water and salts under-
        ground 113, **113**
Charon (Pluto's moon) 21, 22, **22,** 27, 115
ChemCam 113
Chemical weathering 54–55

Chicxulub crater, Mexico **84, 115**
Climate and water 92–101
    climate, defined 94, 115
    Earth 94–95, **94-95**
    Jupiter 99
    Mars 96–97, **96-97,** 100, **100-101**
    Saturn 99, **99**
    Titan 98, **98**
    water cycle 94–95, **95,** 99
Comets **49**
    defined 17, 115
    dust 28
    future research 106, **106**
    hitting Jupiter 82, **82,** 85, 86
    overview **28,** 28–29
    in solar system 18
    water in 49
Compact Reconnaissance
    Imaging Spectrometer for
    Mars (CRISM) 112
Constellations 30, **30, 31,** 115
Convection currents 45, 115
Copernicus, Nicolaus 13
Craters 69, 80–91
    amateur astronomy 82, 87
    counting 86
    defined 82, 115
    density 86
    determining age of planet
        86
    Earth **84,** 85, **85, 90,** 91, **91, 115**
    formation 83, 88–89
    growth 83
    Jupiter 85
    make your own 85
    measuring 75, **75**
    Mimas **87**
    moon 80–81, 83
    parts of 88–89, **88-89**

recurring slope lineae **97**
    size 83, 85
CRISM (Compact
    Reconnaissance Imaging
    Spectrometer for Mars) 112
Cryovolcanoes 46, 115
Curiosity rover **73, 117**
    cost 72
    data collection 76, 78
    defined 117
    landing 77, **77**
    landing site **96,** 105
    launch **71, 76**
    mission 76
    people involved 6, 72, **78-79**
    scientific instruments **74,** 78, 113
    test bed rover **7**

D

Dawn spacecraft 24, 113
Deep Space Network 76
Diamonds, in Saturn's atmo-
    sphere 99
Dwarf planets 18, 22, 23
    see also Ceres; Eris; Haumea;
    Makemake; Pluto

E

Earth (planet)
    asteroid impact **83**
    craters 85, 91, **91, 115**
    defined 115
    distance from sun 18
    erosion and weathering
        52–53
    formation 38
    geysers **46**
    gravity 53
    in habitable zone 10–11, 104, **104**
    meteors 91
    mountain formation **45**
    orbit 19
    overview 38, **38**

plate tectonics 38, 45, **45,** 49, 62
Ring of Fire 62, **62,** 63
rotation 19
in solar system 13, **16,** 17
volcanoes 62, 63, 67, **67**
water cycle 94–95, **95**
water source 49, **49**
Earthquakes 62
Ehlmann, Bethany 6, **6–7,** 112–113, **112**
Enceladus (Saturn's moon) **44**
alien life 110, **110**
defined 115
ice and water 40, **42–43,** 42–46
plate tectonics 45
size 46
surface 42, **42**
travel to 43
Eris (dwarf planet) 13, **16,** 22, 24, **24,** 115
Erosion and weathering 50–59
avalanches 100
chemical weathering 54–55
defined 115
and gravity 53
physical weathering 54
stone formations **53**
Try This 53, 55
Venus **54**
water erosion 52, **52**
wind erosion 51, 52
Europa (Jupiter's moon)
alien life 111, **111**
defined 115
future research 107, **107**
gravity 65
missions to 72
plate tectonics 45, 46, 48, 49
surface 48, **48**
water 44, 45, 46, **47,** 48, 105, 107, **107,** 111
European Space Agency (ESA) 28–29, 57, 70
Everest, Mount, China-Nepal 66
Exploration *see* Space exploration

F
Frost experiment 37

G
Galilei, Galileo 15, 65
Galileo mission 29
Ganymede (Jupiter's moon) 44, 45, 65, 111, **111**
Gas giants (planets) 17, 39, 116
Geysers 42, **46, 47**
Glossary 114–119
Go, Christopher 82
Grand Canyon, Arizona, U.S.A. 52, **52**
Gravity 14-15
defined 116
Earth 53
Jupiter 24, 65
Mars 37
Saturn 40, 46
Titan 56
Gupta, Sanjeev 105, **105**

H
Habitable zone 10–11, 116
Hammel, Heidi 41, **41**
Haumea (dwarf planet) **16,** 22, 25, **25,** 27, 116
Hawaiian Islands 62, 63, 67, **67**
Hayabusa (JAXA spacecraft) **26**
Heights, measuring 75, **75**
Heliocentric solar system 15, **15,** 116
Huygens probe, photo by **57**

I
IAU (International Astronomical Union) 23, 27
IDPs (interplanetary dust particles) 28
Impact craters *see* Craters
Infrared spectrometers 73, 116
International Astronomical Union (IAU) 23, 27
Interplanetary dust particles (IDPs) 28

Io (Jupiter's moon) 60–61, 65, **65**
Itokawa (asteroid) **26**

J
Jupiter (planet) **116**
atmosphere 39, 99
comet impacts 82, **82,** 85, 86
defined 116
distance from sun 18
Galileo mission 29
gravity 24, 65
helium rain 99
missions to 72
orbit 19
overview 39, **39**
red spot 32–33, 39
rotation 19
in solar system **16,** 17

K
Kepler, Johannes 15
Kepler-11 solar system 10, **10**
Kilauea volcano, Hawaii, U.S.A. 63
Kraken Mare, Titan 106, **106**
Kuiper belt
defined 116
dwarf planets **16,** 18, 22, 25
location 18
New Horizons flyby 21, 23
perturbations 13

L
Lasers 74, **74**
Laws of planetary motion 15
Levy, David 86
Life
habitable zone 10–11
ingredients for 11, 46
likely places 110–111, **110-111**
protection from Earthlings 70
search for 108
Lonar crater, India 91

Lopes, Rosaly 66, **66**
Lunar Reconnaissance Orbiter **72, 118**

M

Magma 62-63, 116
Makemake (dwarf planet) **16,** 22, 25, **25,** 27, 116
Manicouagan crater, Quebec, Canada **90,** 91
Mars (planet)
    alien life 110, **110**
    atmosphere 36–37, 58
    avalanches 100, **101**
    channels **52,** 58, **95,** 96, 105
    craters 86, 88–89, **88–89**
    dark rock **59**
    defined 117
    distance from sun 18
    future research 107, **107, 108**
    in habitable zone 10–11
    humans on 37, **37,** 107, **107, 108**
    lake water 97, 113, **113**
    MAVEN spacecraft **70**
    in meteorites 66
    Nili Fossae region 112, **112**
    Olympus Mons 66, **66**
    overview 36–37
    Oxia Palus region **36**
    planetary geomorphology 58
    polar ice caps 8–9, 37, **100**
    rovers 71, **73** (see also Curiosity rover)
    sand **59**
    in solar system **16,** 17
    spectroscopy 96–97
    surface water 44, 92–93
    Tharsis Montes region 66
    underground water **96,** 97, 112, **112**
    volcanoes 66, **66**
Mars Exploration Rover (MER) 71
Mars Reconnaissance Orbiter (MRO) 92–93

Mars Science Lab (MSL) **71, 76,** 76–79
MAVEN spacecraft **70**
Mercury (planet) **16,** 17, 18, 19, **34,** 34–35, **35,** 117
MESSENGER probe **34,** 35
Meteor showers 28, 117
Meteorites 26, **26,** 66, 81, 83, 91
Meteoroids **29,** 117
Meteors **29,** 81, 91, 117
    see also Craters
Milky Way galaxy 30, 117
Mimas (Saturn's moon) **87, 121**
Mission sequence 72
Moon
    age 86
    dark side 8–9
    defined 117
    exploration 72, **72,** 73, **118**
    formation 38
    impact craters 80–81, 83
Moon Mineralogy Mapper 73
Mountains, measuring 75, **75**
MRO (Mars Reconnaissance Orbiter) 92–93
MSL (Mars Science Lab) **71, 76,** 76–79

N

NASA
    Deep Space Network 76
    defined 117
    future plans 106–107, **106–107**
    mission statement 70
    see also specific missions and spacecraft
Nebulae 14, **14,** 15, 117
Neptune (planet)
    defined 117
    distance from sun 18
    orbit 19
    overview 41, **41**
    in solar system **16,** 17
    water 44
New Horizons space probe 20–21, 23, 72

Nili Fossae region, Mars 112, **112**
Nitrogen 108, 117

O

Old Faithful, Yellowstone National Park, U.S.A. 46, **46**
Olympus Mons, Mars 66, **66**
Oort cloud 18, 28, 117
Opportunity rover 71, **73,** 97

P

Perseid meteor shower 28
Photosphere 17, 118
Physical weathering 54
Pieters, Carle 73, **73**
Pingos 58
Planet Nine **12,** 13, 118
Planetary motion, laws of 15
Planetesimals 14, **14,** 15, 118
Planets 32–41
    age determination 86
    defined 22, 118
    distance from sun 18
    formation 14, **14,** 15
    orbits 19
    search for 12, **12**
    solar system **11, 16**
    TRAPPIST-1 system **11**
    see also specific planets
Plate tectonics
    defined 45, 118
    Earth 38, 45, **45,** 49, 62
    Europa 45, 46, 48, 49
    how it works 48
    recycling crust 49
    and volcanoes 62
Pluto (dwarf planet)
    classification 13, 18, 22, 23
    defined 118
    exploration 20–21, 23, 72
    moons 22, **22**
    name 22, 27
    north pole **18**
    overview 23, **23**
    in solar system **16,** 22
Power systems 71

Propulsion systems 71, 118
Ptolemy 13

R

Radar mapping 72–73
Recurring slope lineae **97**
Ring of Fire, Earth 62, **62**, 63
Rosetta comet mission 28–29

S

Sample Analysis at Mars (SAM)
  instrument **74**
Sand dunes 56, **57**, 58
Saturn (planet)
    Cassini-Huygens
      Spacecraft 58
    defined 118
    diamonds in atmosphere
      99
    distance from sun 18
    gravity 40, 46
    moons 27, 33, 42, **42**, 44,
      45, 46
    overview 40, **40**
    rings 33, 40, **40**, 121
    in solar system **16**, 17
Shadows, for measurement
  75, **75**
Shoemaker, Carolyn 86
Shoemaker, Eugene 86, **86**
Shoemaker-Levy 9 comet
  85, 86
67P/Churyumov-Gerasimenko
  (comet) 29
Sky Crane 77, **77**
Sojourner rover **73**
Solar system
    age 86
    center 13, 15
    Copernicus's model **13**
    fastest spinning object 26
    football-field-size model 18
    formation 14, **14**, 15
    habitable zone 10–11
    Planet Nine **12**, 13
    planets **11, 12, 16**
Solar winds 17, 58

Space exploration 68–75
    countries involved in 70
    exploring from afar 72–73
    measuring heights 75, **75**
    mission planning 71
    mission sequence 72
    shooting lasers 74, **74**
Spectroscopy 73, 96–97, 112–
  113, **112-113**, 116, 119
Spider crater, Australia 91, **91**
Spirit (Mars rover) 54, 71, **73**
Stardust mission 28
Stars 30, **30**
Sun 13, 14, **14**, 15, 17, 34
Supernovae 30, 119, **119**
Swift-Tuttle comet 28

T

Tectonic plates *see* Plate
  tectonics
Titan (Saturn's moon)
    alien life 110, **110**
    atmosphere 56, 58
    cryovolcano 46
    future research 106, **106**
    gravity 56
    lakes and seas 98, **98**,
      106, **106**
    methane 51, 58, 98
    name 27
    sand dunes 56, **57**, 58
    windstorm 50–51
TRAPPIST-1 solar system 10,
  11, 111, **111**
2008 HJ (asteroid) 26

U

Uranus (planet)
    defined 119
    distance from sun 18
    overview 41, **41**
    rotation 19, 41
    in solar system **16**, 17
    water 44
Ursa Major (constellation) **31**
Ursa Minor (constellation) 30

V

Venus (planet)
    atmosphere 36, 64
    defined 119
    distance from sun 18
    future research 107, **107**
    in habitable zone 10–11,
      111, **111**
    Lavinia Planitia region **54**
    overview 36–37
    radar image **36**
    rotation 19
    in solar system **16**, 17
    surface **54**
    temperature 36, 111
    volcanoes 64–65, **64-65**
Visual and InfraRed (VIR)
  Mapping Spectrometer 113
Volcanoes 60–67
    cryovolcanoes 46, 115
    Earth 62, 63, 67, **67**
    formation 62
    and gravity 65
    Io 60–61, 65, **65**
    Mars 66, **66**
    and plate tectonics 62
    Ring of Fire, Earth 62, **62**
    types of 63, **63**
    Venus 64–65, **64-65**
    volcanic vent 119
Vostok, Lake, Antarctica
  105, **105**
Vredefort crater, South Africa
  85

W

Wadhwa, Meenakshi 26, **26**
Water and climate *see* Climate
  and water
Water cycle 94–95, **95**, 99
Weathering *see* Erosion and
  weathering
Wesley, Anthony 82
Wild 2 (comet) 28, **28**

CREDITS

Cover, Ben Shannon; (Background), Photojogtom/Dreamstime; 2-3, (Background) Photojogtom/Dreamstime; 4-5, Inigo Cia/Getty Images; 6 (UP), Courtesy of Bethany Ehlmann; 6 (CTR), Courtesy of Bethany Ehlmann; 6 (LO), Courtesy of Bethany Ehlmann; 7, Courtesy of Bethany Ehlmann; 10, NASA/Ames/JPL-Caltech; 11 (UP), Science Photo Library/Getty Images; 11 (LO), NASA/JPL-Caltech; 12, Smilyk Pavel/Shutterstock; 13 (UP), Shannon Stirone; 13 (LO), Marka/UIG via Getty Images; 14, David Aguilar; 16, David Aguilar; 18, NASA/Johns Hopkins University Applied Physics Laboratory/Southwest Research Institute; 22, NASA/Johns Hopkins University Applied Physics Laboratory/Southwest Research Institute; 23, NASA/Johns Hopkins University Applied Physics Laboratory/Southwest Research Institute; 24 (UP), NASA/JPL-Caltech; 24 (LO), NASA/JPL-Caltech/UCLA/MPS/DLR/IDA; 25 (UP), NASA; 25 (LO), NASA/JPL-Caltech/R. Hurt (SSC-Caltech); 26 (LE), Arizona State University; 26 (RT), Akihiro Ikeshita/AFP/Getty Images; 27, Luc Novovitch/Alamy Stock Photo; 27 (Inset), IMG Stock Studio/Shutterstock; 28, NASA/JPL-Caltech; 29 (UP), Ali Ihsan Ozturk/Anadolu Agency/Getty Images; 29 (LO), NASA/JPL; 30 (UP), Babak Tafreshi/National Geographic Creative; 30 (1), Becky Hale/NG Staff; 30 (2), Becky Hale/NG Staff; 30 (5), Becky Hale/NG Staff; 30 (7), Becky Hale/NG Staff; 31, Dan Mitchell/Getty Images; 34 (LE), NASA/JPL/Malin Space Science Systems; 34 (RT), NASA/Johns Hopkins University Applied Physics Laboratory/Carnegie Institution of Washington; 35, NASA/JHU-APL/ASU/Carnegie Institution of Washington/Science Photo Library; 36 (UP), NASA/JPL/USGS; 36 (LO), NASA/JPL/USGS; 37, Jim Olive/Polaris/Newscom; 38, Ali Ender Birer/Dreamstime; 39, NASA/JPL/Space Science Institute; 40, NASA/JPL-Caltech/SSI; 41 (UP), Courtesy Heidi Hammel; 41 (LE), NASA/JPL/Lawrence Sromovsky, University of Wisconsin–Madison/W.W. Keck Observatory; 41 (RT), NASA/JPL; 44, NASA/JPL/Space Science Institute; 45, Irakite/Dreamstime; 46, Photodisc; 47, NASA/ESA/K. Retherford/SWRI; 48, Stocktrek/Getty Images; 49, johan63/Getty Images; 52 (UP), Michele Falzone/Getty Images; 52 (LO), ESA/DLR/FU Berlin; 53, Stefano Buttafoco/Shutterstock; 54 (UP), NASA/JPL/Cornell; 54 (LO), NASA/JSC; 55, Rinusbaak/Dreamstime; 56, Courtesy of Devon Burr/UTK; 57 (UP), ESA/NASA/JPL/University of Arizona; 57 (LO LE), NASA/JPL-Caltech/ASI; 57 (LO RT), NASA; 58, Courtesy of Devon Burr/UTK; 59 (UP), NASA/JPL-Caltech/Univ. of Arizona; 59 (LO), NASA/JPL/University of Arizona; 62, Steve and Donna O'Meara/National Geographic Creative; 63 (UP), Azuzl/Shutterstock; 63 (CTR), ttsz/Getty Images; 63 (LO), ttsz/Getty Images; 64, World History Archive/Alamy Stock Photo; 65, SSPL/Getty Images; 66 (UP), NASA/JPL; 66 (LO), Kees Veenenbos/Science Source; 67, Stocktrek Images/Getty Images;

ACKNOWLEDGMENTS ● ● ● ● ● ● ● ● ●

Thanks to my family for nurturing my early curiosity about the world and to my teachers and mentors who helped me turn that love into a career in exploration. I greatly appreciate the hard work of the editors and staff at National Geographic, especially Shelby Alinsky, and my amazing co-author Jennifer Swanson. It takes a village to make a book, and it's been fun to be a part of this team. —BE

To Susan Roth, my 7th grade science teacher, who opened my eyes to the amazing intrigue and adventure that the world of science has to offer. She is my true Science Superhero. —JS

The authors and publisher also wish to thank the book team: Shelby Alinsky, Kathryn Williams, Grace Hill Smith, Julide Dengel, Sarah J. Mock, Joan Gossett, Gus Tello, Joe Levit, Ben Shannon, Jeff Heimsath, and Girl Friday Productions.

Since 1888, the National Geographic Society has funded more than 12,000 research, exploration, and preservation projects around the world. The Society receives funds from National Geographic Partners, LLC, funded in part by your purchase. A portion of the proceeds from this book supports this vital work. To learn more, visit natgeo.com/info.

NATIONAL GEOGRAPHIC and Yellow Border Design are trademarks of the National Geographic Society, used under license.

For more information, visit nationalgeographic.com, call 1-800-647-5463, or write to the following address:

National Geographic Partners
1145 17th Street N.W.
Washington, D.C. 20036-4688 U.S.A.

Visit us online at nationalgeographic.com/books
For librarians and teachers: ngchildrensbooks.org
More for kids from National Geographic: kids.nationalgeographic.com

For information about special discounts for bulk purchases, please contact National Geographic Books Special Sales: specialsales@natgeo.com

For rights or permissions inquiries, please contact National Geographic Books Subsidiary Rights: bookrights@natgeo.com

Library of Congress Cataloging-in-Publication Data

Names: Ehlmann, Bethany, author. | Swanson, Jennifer, author.
Title: Dr. E's super stellar solar system / by Dr. Bethany Ehlmann
    and Jennifer Swanson.
Description: Washington, DC : National Geographic Kids, [2018] |
Audience: Age 9-12. | Audience: Grade 4 to 6. | Includes index.
Identifiers: LCCN 2017020438| ISBN 9781426327988 (paperback) |
    ISBN 9781426327995 (hardcover)
Subjects: LCSH: Solar system--Juvenile literature.
Classification: LCC QB501.3 .E35 2018 | DDC 523.2--dc23
LC record available at https://lccn.loc.gov/2017020438

Printed in China
17/RRDS/1